KETO *in an*

INSTANT

100   KETOGENIC RECIPES FOR YOUR INSTANT POT®

KETO in an INSTANT

100 KETOGENIC RECIPES FOR YOUR INSTANT POT®

Use of the trademarks is authorized by Instant Brands Inc., owner of Instant Pot®

STACEY CRAWFORD

CONTENTS

ABOUT THE AUTHOR

Stacey Crawford is the owner of beautyandthefoodie.com where she creates and shares healthy, low-carb, ketogenic recipes. As a sufferer of celiac disease, she's discovered that eating healthy, satisfying food through a grain-free, low-carb ketogenic diet is the key to creating good health. As a licensed cosmetologist, she also creates natural beauty products and natural home health remedies.

ACKNOWLEDGMENTS

I would like to thank the DK Publishing team for choosing me to work on this project. They made this challenging learning experience a pleasant one.

A special thanks to the editor, Brook Farling, who patiently guided and helped me through the whole process and organized everything. He is an absolute joy to work with.

To my mom, Sandra, and dad, Neil, for encouraging me in all my endeavors.

To my Aunt Kathy, who is my favorite author and role model. You have been a positive and caring influence in my life.

To Jennifer Eloff for teaching, mentoring, and inspiring me during my low-carb journey. You always advised me, believed in me, and encouraged me from the very beginning.

To my husband Don, who is my rock, a pillar of support, and my biggest cheerleader in all things for over 30 years. Your endless love and support have enabled me to accomplish more than I ever thought possible.

And to my kids, Danielle, Raul, and Hunter for encouraging me, believing in me, and taste testing all my recipes and food experiments.

INTRODUCTION

When I first discovered the ketogenic diet, I thought it would be just another fad diet or temporary weight loss solution. I had tried so many different diets in the past (at the time I was over 40), yet none of the diets I tried seemed to give me results. I was utterly frustrated with being hungry, counting calories, and exercising to the point of exhaustion or injury. As a last resort, I decided to try the ketogenic low-carb diet, merely because it was the only one I hadn't tried yet. Thinking that the diet would inevitably fail, I was astonished that I lost weight, saw clearer skin, and gained extra energy while enjoying delicious foods without any hunger. I'm in my fifties now and could not be happier with the ketogenic lifestyle, as I feel even better than I did in my twenties. I genuinely feel like I've found the fountain of youth.

Discovering the Instant Pot, a popular and multifunctional appliance, was a game changer for me. The Instant Pot makes cooking healthy ketogenic meals easier and faster, and with fewer dishes to wash. The keto diet, with the help of the Instant Pot, is a winning combination that makes eating healthy a breeze.

This book will give you the basics on how to start a ketogenic diet, count your net carbs, and use your Instant Pot, and it includes 100 healthy, flavorful, ketogenic recipes to prepare in the Instant Pot. I want this to be a resource and tool for you so that you will have everything you need to start a ketogenic lifestyle with your Instant Pot.

KETO
BASICS

WHAT IS THE KETOGENIC DIET?

The ketogenic diet is a high-fat, moderate-protein, low-carbohydrate diet that can produce significant health benefits for both the mind and body. Keto is not a new concept, but recently it's been embraced as a better way to burn fat, lose weight, and improve health. But what is it, and how did it come about?

ORIGINS OF THE KETO DIET

Physicians first introduced the ketogenic diet in the early twentieth century as a treatment for managing seizure symptoms in epilepsy patients. Prior to the discovery of the keto diet, physicians commonly prescribed fasting as a treatment for reducing seizures. And while fasting produced some positive results, it simply was not a sustainable way to eat. It was later discovered that patients who ate a high-fat, low-carbohydrate diet often experienced the same metabolic effects that fasting had produced, but without the need for prolonged fasting. Recent scientific studies on the impact of the ketogenic diet show significant health benefits including improved brain function, decreased insulin resistance, lower blood sugar levels, weight loss, and more. Eating high levels of dietary fat was once considered taboo, but science is proving it to be a smarter and more sustainable way to fuel your body and improve your health.

KETOSIS AND MACRONUTRIENTS

The key to success on the ketogenic diet is consuming the right types of foods in the proper ratios to force your body into a metabolic state called *ketosis.* Ketosis occurs when the body is so starved of the sugars it typically utilizes for fuel—sugars that normally come from sugar and carbohydrates—that it's instead forced to burn existing body fat to produce fuel. A by-product of this process are *ketones,* which are the organic compunds the body uses for fuel in place of glucose. Ketones are produced by the liver through ketosis and are measurable in the body when a state of ketosis is achieved.

The key to attaining ketosis is consuming the right balance of macronutrients. These core macros—protein, fat, and carbohydrates—are all found in the foods we eat and are the benchmarks for measuring the nutritional breakdown of a diet. A typical western diet has about 25 to 35 percent of calories coming from fat, 15 to 25 percent from protein, and 50 to 60 percent from carbohydrates. The ketogenic diet, however, generally has around 70 to 75 percent of calories coming from fat, 15 to 20 percent from protein, and only about 5 to 10 percent from carbohydrates. Most keto dieters follow this general macro ratio, although there are some variations—athletes, for instance, may consume more carbs for fuel and to aid in recovery.

CARBS AND NET CARBS

Carbohydrates are compounds that are present in most of the foods we eat and they're what the body uses to produce glucose, which in turn is what it uses for fuel. There are different types of carbs, including simple carbohydrates and complex carbohydrates. Simple carbs are comprised of simple sugars or starches and are what the body converts into glucose, which it then uses as energy or stores away as fat. Complex carbs are more difficult for the body to digest and thus don't create the spikes in blood sugar that simple carbs produce, so they're a much less efficient source of energy for the body. While simple carbs are converted into energy quickly, they raise blood sugar levels and can be converted into fat. Complex carbs, and fiber, generally do not raise blood sugar levels, are less digestible, and are not converted into fat. (Fiber is also a form of carbohydrate, but unlike simple carbs, fiber is not digestible, so it's not usable as a source of energy and instead is just passed through the body.)

Net carbs, which are what are reflected in the recipes in this book, represent a more accurate measurement of the actual number of digestible carbohydrates in a recipe, as opposed to all carbs. Calculating net carbs is a helpful way to more accurately measure the impact of carbs and fiber on your daily macros, and they're simple to calculate: simply subtract the total grams of fiber from the total grams of carbohydrates in a food to get the total net carbs. On a keto diet, your intake of net carbs will be limited to about 20 to 50 grams per day.

What does a keto diet plate look like?

A typical keto plate will include proteins, such as beef, poultry, seafood, fish, or eggs, covered in a high-fat sauce or butter, with sides of lower-carb, high-fiber vegetables covered in melted butter, cheese, or high-fat sauces or dressings.

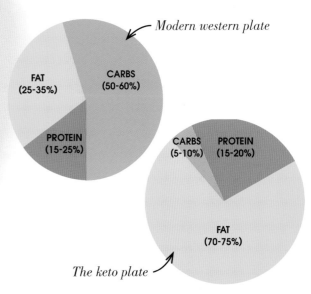

Modern western plate

FAT
(25-35%)

CARBS
(50-60%)

PROTEIN
(15-25%)

CARBS
(5-10%)

PROTEIN
(15-20%)

FAT
(70-75%)

The keto plate

WHAT CAN YOU EAT?

Following a ketogenic diet means you'll be eating a significantly higher percentage of healthy fats, while eating a reasonable amount of protein and consuming only a very small ratio of carbohydrates that will come primarily from lower carb fruits and vegetables. You'll be eating richer, more satisfying foods that will nourish your body and give you more sustained energy throughout the day. And since you won't be using carbs for fuel, you'll stay feeling full for longer since your body burns fat slower than it can burn carbs.

On a ketogenic diet you'll eat foods like eggs; meats; fish; seafood; lower-carb nuts (such as pecans, walnuts, and almonds); healthy oils; butter; cheeses; heavy cream; non-starchy high-fiber, low-carb vegetables; and lower sugar fruits, such as berries. Foods you'll avoid include sugary, high-carb, highly processed foods such as grains; pasta; bread;

white or wheat flour; rice; oats; potatoes; corn; beans; quinoa; starchy vegetables; and higher-carb fruits. The fast-burning carbs contained in these foods can cause elevated blood sugar levels and weight gain, and also create a higher risk of obesity as well as developing type 2 diabetes. Consuming these foods will also prevent your body from entering ketosis.

Many keto dieters prefer to calculate very specific macro percentages to determine how many calories of fat, protein, and carbohydrates they should be eating. If you're struggling to achieve your goals, you may find that you need to calculate your specific macro needs based on factors including your age, weight, and body fat percentage, as well as other factors. The calculation for determining personal macro percentages is fairly complex, so it's best to use an online keto macro calculator to get a more customized macro percentage. (A simple online calculator can be found on my website.)

HOW DOES KETOSIS WORK?

How your body generates energy—and how it uses that energy—is a direct result of the foods you eat, how your body processes those foods, and how your health is impacted, as a result. Ketosis is a metabolic state where the body is forced to consume existing body fat for fuel because it's being starved of glucose, which is the normal source of fuel on a high-carbohydrate diet.

HOW YOUR BODY CREATES FUEL ON A HIGH-CARB DIET

On a standard western diet a large amount of carbohydrates are consumed, which the body then utilizes as a source of fuel for energy. The digestive system breaks down these carbohydrates and turns them into glucose molecules, which then go into the bloodstream and on to the organs and muscles where they are used as energy.

Once consumed, carbohydrates are metabolized by the body very quickly, providing quick burning fuel and a short-term burst of energy. But because this type of energy is short-lived, it only provides energy and satiety for a short amount of time, and thus the body becomes starved for more fuel in a shorter period of time. This is why we commonly feel hungrier sooner on a high-carb diet, and is also why our energy stores are depleted faster (commonly referred to as low blood sugar or a *sugar crash*).

High-carb diets can also elevate blood sugar levels, which can cause the pancreas to produce more insulin to counter the excess glucose. These increases in insulin can eventually cause the body's cells to become resistant to insulin, and thus elevate the individual risk of developing type 2 diabetes.

1 A high-carbohydrate food is consumed.

2 The pancreas generates insulin, which allows the glucose—or blood sugar—to be utilized for energy.

3 Small, unused quantities of glucose are converted to glycogen and stored in the muscles and liver for later use.

4 The remaining glucose is used by the body for energy. Any excess glucose that is not burned for energy is then converted into stored body fat.

HOW YOUR BODY CREATES FUEL ON A KETO DIET

On a ketogenic diet there isn't enough glucose for the body to use as energy, so it will then burn fat stores to produce an alternate form of energy, which the liver then breaks down to make energy. During this process, ketones are formed as a byproduct and are what the body eventually uses for energy. Because dietary fats are metabolized by the body at a slower rate than carbs, you will feel satiated for longer periods of time while enjoying longer lasting energy. Once ketosis is achieved, eventually you will experience increased energy levels increased mental clarity, better sleep, and improved congitive function. (Note that when your body first enters ketosis, you may experience some temporary adverse effects including bad breath, odd-smelling urine, and fatigue. Often called "keto flu," the unpleasant symptoms of this condition will subside as your body adapts to the changes it's experiencing.)

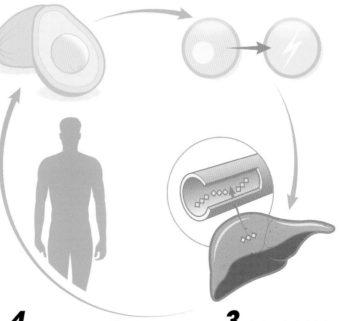

1 A high-fat, low-carb food is consumed.

2 Due to the absence of sugars in the consumed food, the body burns stored body fat to create energy.

4 Ketones are utilized by the body for energy. Excess ketones are expelled through the kidneys and lungs.

3 As body fat is broken down, the liver produces ketones, which are then sent back into the body though the bloodstream.

Ketoacidosis and ketosis—know the difference

Although they sound similar, ketosis and ketoacidosis—also known as diabetic ketoacidosis—are not the same. Ketoacidosis is a life-threatening complication of type 1 diabetes caused by excessively high levels of ketones in the liver and elevated blood sugar levels. It can occur in people with type 2 diabetes or alcoholism, and can occur as a result of inadequate insulin levels in a person with diabetes, or as a result of an improper diet. It can also occur during periods of extreme starvation. A healthy, low-carb diet with properly managed ketones does not cause ketoacidosis. Ketosis is not harmful and is just a sign of the presence of an elevated level of ketones in the blood and urine. Although ketosis does produce ketones, it does not cause high enough levels of ketones to cause ketoacidosis.

Signs and symptoms of ketoacidosis

> Frequent urination
> Extreme thirst
> Nausea and vomiting
> Abdominal pain
> Confusion
> Difficulty breathing
> Lethargy

Note: Prior to making any significant changes to your diet, it's recommended that you consult with a physician to have a complete physical check-up, have your blood sugar tested, and be screened for any other health issues. If you experience any symptoms of ketoacidosis, you should stop the diet immediately and see a doctor to get tested. In severe cases of ketoacidosis, you should seek emergency medical assistance immediately.

THE KETOGENIC KITCHEN

Knowing what you can eat—and what to avoid—is an important step in getting started with a keto diet. The following guide will help you understand which foods are keto-friendly and which should be avoided.

GOOD

VEGETABLES
alfalfa sprouts, artichokes, arugula, asparagus, avocado, bell pepper, bok choy, broccoli, Brussels sprouts, cabbage, cauliflower, celery, chili peppers, collard greens, cucumber, eggplant, endive, garlic, green beans, green onion, iceberg lettuce, jalapeño, jicama, kale, mushrooms, mustard greens, okra, olives, pumpkin, radishes, spinach, squash, Swiss chard, tomatoes, tomatillos, turnips, watercress, zucchini

FRUITS
blackberries, blueberries, coconut (unsweetened), lemon, lime, raspberries, strawberries

FATS AND OILS
avocado oil, bacon grease, butter, coconut oil, ghee, lard, nut and seed oils, olive oil, palm shortening, sesame oil

MEAT AND EGGS
beef, eggs, fish, pork, poultry, seafood and shellfish

DAIRY
full-fat butter, full-fat cheeses (hard, soft, semisoft cream cheeses, ricotta, and mascarpone), full-fat sour cream, heavy cream (whipping cream)

DAIRY-FREE ALTERNATIVES
almond cheese, unsweetened almond milk, unsweetened full-fat coconut cream, unsweetened full-fat coconut milk

IN MODERATION

VEGETABLES
carrots, celeriac root, onions, rutabagas

FRUITS
cantaloupe, cherries, clementines, kiwi, peaches, plums, watermelon

MEAT AND EGGS
uncured or minimally processed meats that have no sugar added and are gluten and nitrate-free, including bacon, ham, sausage, pepperoni, salami, hot dogs, and some deli meats

DAIRY AND DAIRY-FREE ALTERNATIVES
full-fat cottage cheese, full-fat unsweetened plain Greek yogurt

AVOID

VEGETABLES
beets, corn, parsnips, peas, potatoes, sweet potatoes, yams

FRUITS
apples, bananas, dates (and most other dried fruits), grapes, mangoes, oranges, pears, pineapple

FATS AND OILS
fully hydrogenated oils (peanut, corn, cottonseed), grapeseed oil, partially hydrogenated oils (palm, vegetable, canola, soybean), margarine, processed vegetable oils

MEAT AND EGGS
Processed meats that contain additives such as sugar, corn syrup, maple syrup, wheat flour, rice flour, or other starches

DAIRY AND DAIRY-FREE ALTERNATIVES
dairy milks (nonfat, low-fat, and whole varieties as they contain sugars), nonfat or low-fat dairy products that contain added sugars, sweetened coconut milk, sweetened nut milks (including almond and cashew), sweetened yogurts, yogurts containing high-carb fruits (such as apples or bananas), sugar-sweetened dairy desserts (including ice cream, frozen yogurt, and milkshakes)

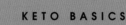

SWEETENERS

GOOD

Erythritol and oligosaccharide blends (such as Swerve)—This is a sugar alcohol and fiber blend that comes in granular and confectioners' styles. It's calorie-free, low glycemic, has non-impact carbs (which means the carbs in it are not metabolized), and it does not raise blood sugar levels. It tastes similar to sugar and measures the same as sugar. It can also brown or caramelize like sugar, which makes it an ideal sweetener blend for baking.

Erythritol and stevia blends (such as Truvia)—A sugar alcohol and stevia blend that is low carb. This sweetener blend also works well for baking, but it is sweeter than sugar. If using this blend, you may need to check the packaging for conversion ratios when using this option to replace other sweeteners.

Stevia and inulin blends (such as Sweet Leaf)—A granular, low carb stevia and fiber combination sweetener. Good for coffee, tea, whipped cream, or yogurt, but not the best for baking.

Stevia—A low-carb sweetener that is available in granular and liquid forms. Works well in liquids or cold foods, but not well for baking. Stevia is a concentrated herb that can have a strong aftertaste. It's usually better tasting when blended with sugar alcohol.

Monk fruit—A more difficult-to-find low-carb sweetener that can be low carb, depending on the brand and what other ingredients are in it.

Xylitol—A sugar alcohol low-carb sweetener option. (Note that it is very toxic to dogs and also has been known to cause gastric issues for some people.)

AVOID

agave syrup, coconut sugar, date sugar, fruit juices, high-fructose corn syrup, honey, maple syrup, sugar (white, brown, or raw)

Any artificial sweeteners such as aspartame, saccharin, and sucralose (although low carb, the health risks outweigh the benefits)

SPECIALTY INGREDIENTS

• **Unsweetened almond milk and coconut milk**—These unsweetened nut milks are lower in carbs than traditional dairy milk.

• **Coconut cream**—A solid cream made from coconut milk and a dairy-free alternative to whipped heavy cream

• **Coconut flour**—A low-carb, high-fiber, high-fat, and gluten-free flour made from dried and ground coconut meat. Used in low-carb baking.

• **Almond flour**—A low-carb, high-fat, gluten-free flour made from ground almonds. Used in low-carb baking.

• **Golden flaxseed meal**—A low-carb, high-fiber, gluten-free seed meal used in low-carb baking.

• **Arrowroot powder**—A starchy root powder that, when used in small amounts, is good for thickening sauces and soups. (Note that arrowroot powder is not low carb and should be used only in small quantities.)

• **Xanthan gum**—A natural emulsifier and thickener that is used to thicken sauces or creams, or to help bind gluten-free flours in baking.

Baking with low-carb sweeteners

When baking with low-carb sweeteners, always try to use the exact sweetener called for in the recipe. Changing the sweetener may yield disappointing results and the finished product may not brown properly. If you do need to use a sweetener or sweetener blend that is different than what is called for in the recipe, refer to the brand's conversion charts to make any necessary adjustments to the measurements.

COOKING WITH THE INSTANT POT

Understanding how the Instant Pot works, and how cooking times impact recipe preparation, will help save you time and also help yield better results in the pot. You might also benefit from owning a few extra accessories.

INSTANT POT CONTROLS

- **Program keys**—These are preprogrammed cooking modes, each designed to cook specific types of foods using preset times and pressure levels. Some keys may differ depending on which model you own, but it's important to note that for the main pressure cooking mode some models will have a **Pressure Cook** key, while others will have a **Manual** key.

- **Operation keys**—These enable you to control a number of functions, including adjusting pressure levels, shutting off the pot (by selecting **Cancel**), selecting the **Keep Warm** mode, or selecting **Delay Start** to set a delay time before a cooking cycle starts.

- **Pressure indicator**—Indicates the current pressure level for each of the pressure cooking modes.

- **Mode Indicator**—Lets you adjust the pressure levels from **Less, Normal,** or **More** for each of the various pressure cooking programs.

- **+/- keys**— Each program has a preset cook time, and these enable you to manually adjust the cook times.

- **Time display**—Displays the cook time on the LED screen. When a mode is active, the timer will count down. When a mode is complete and the **Stay Warm** mode has been activated, the display will count up.

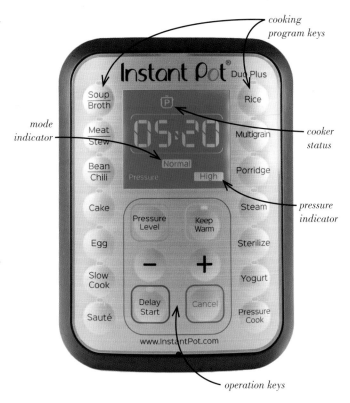

cooking program keys

mode indicator

cooker status

pressure indicator

operation keys

Understanding cooking times in the Instant Pot

Understanding how the different cooking times work will help you better plan your meal times.

- **Prep time**—The amount of time it takes to prepare any ingredients, prior to adding them to the pot for cooking.

- **Build time**—Much like the preheating time in an oven, this is the time it takes for the pressure to build in the pot. The build time is part of every pressure cooking program, but is not included in the actual cook time. (Note that the timer on the pot does not begin until the pot has reached full pressure.)

- **Pressure time**—The time it takes to cook a food once full pressure has been achieved in the pot. Pressure time does not include build, release, or cooling times in the pot.

HANDY ACCESSORIES TO OWN

These accessories are not included with the Instant Pot, but they are used in many of the recipes in this book.

Tempered glass lid

Vented glass lids are not critical to have but many models are made to fit the Instant Pot and they're useful during the slow cooker or yogurt program modes when pressure is not used during the cooking process.

Springform pan

A springform pan is useful when making cakes, cheesecakes, and other recipes in the Instant Pot. Look for a 6-inch (15.25cm) to 7-inch (17.5cm) pan that will easily fit inside the inner pot. A nonstick model will help minimize cleanup.

Silicone muffin cups

Reusable, washable silicone muffin or cupcake liner cups are easy to clean and very handy for making muffins or cupcakes in the Instant Pot.

Steamer basket

A steamer basket is useful for steaming items that don't fit well on the steam rack. Look for a stainless steel or silicone model with legs and small holes, which will allow steam to circulate, and in a size that will fit inside the pot.

Ramekins

Ramekins are useful for cooking items in the Instant Pot that are portioned into single servings, such as desserts. Look for heavy-duty ceramic ramekins that come in 4oz (110ml) and 6oz (170ml) sizes.

- **Release time**—The time it takes for the pot to release the pressure once the cook time is complete. This can happen either by natural release, which means the pressure is allowed to release naturally, or by quick release, which means the pressure is forced from the pot by flipping the steam release handle on the lid. Quick release can take as little as 1 minute, while natural release can take as long as 30 minutes, depending on food temperature, volume of food in the pot, and other factors.

- **Total time**—The time it should take to complete a recipe from start to finish, beginning with the preparation of any ingredients to the point at which the recipe is ready to be served. The total time in a recipe includes the prep time, build time, cook or pressure times, release time, and time for any other steps that may be required to complete the recipe such as sautéing, resting, chilling, marinating, or setting.

BREAKFAST

SERVES: 8
SERVING SIZE: 1 SLICE

PREP: 5 MINUTES
PRESSURE: 22 MINUTES
TOTAL: 41 MINUTES

SETTING: PRESSURE COOK
RELEASE: NATURAL/QUICK

1½ tbsp olive oil

½ cup chopped fresh spinach

5 slices cooked bacon, chopped

5 large eggs

½ cup liquid egg whites

½ cup whole milk ricotta cheese

¼ tsp ground mustard

½ tsp fine grind sea salt

¼ tsp ground black pepper

1 medium tomato, cut into 6 slices

½ cup shredded cheddar cheese

tip *If using a springform pan, make sure to cover the underside of the pan with a sheet of aluminum foil to prevent leakage.*

BACON SPINACH TOMATO FRITTATA

Crust-free and extremely low in carbs, this savory and colorful frittata is loaded with flavorful bacon and fresh spinach. The addition of ricotta cheese helps make this frittata extra fluffy and creamy.

1 Brush a 6 x 3-inch (15.25 x 7.5cm) round soufflé pan with the olive oil. Layer the spinach on the bottom of the pan, followed by the bacon. Set aside.

2 In a large bowl, combine the eggs, egg whites, ricotta cheese, ground mustard, sea salt, and black pepper. Whisk until well blended and no lumps remain.

3 Pour the egg mixture over the spinach and bacon. Arrange the tomato slices on top of the egg mixture. Tightly cover the pan with a sheet of aluminum foil.

4 Place the steam rack in the inner pot and add 2 cups water to the bottom of the pot. Lower the covered pan onto the steam rack.

5 Cover, lock the lid, and flip the steam release handle to the sealing position. Select **Pressure Cook (High)** and set the cook time for **22 minutes.**

6 While the frittata is cooking, preheat the oven broiler to 450°F (232°C).

7 When the cook time for the fritatta is complete, allow the pressure to release naturally for 10 minutes and then quick release the remaining pressure.

8 Open the lid, carefully grasp the steam rack handles, and lift the rack and pan out of the pot. Remove and discard the foil and sprinkle the cheddar over top of the frittata.

9 Place the frittata in the oven and broil for 2–4 minutes, or until the cheese is browned.

10 Remove the frittata from the oven and transfer to a serving platter. Cut into 8 equal-sized wedges. Serve hot.

Nutrition per serving
CALORIES: 155 **FAT:** 12g **NET CARBS:** 2g **PROTEIN:** 11g

SERVES: 4
SERVING SIZE:
1 CUP WITH 1 TBSP SAUCE

PREP: 2 MINUTES
PRESSURE: 3 MINUTES
TOTAL: 7 MINUTES

SETTING: PRESSURE COOK
RELEASE: NATURAL/QUICK

4 large eggs

4 medium bell peppers,
tops and seeds removed

6 baby arugula leaves

FOR THE SAUCE

¼ cup mayonnaise

1 tsp Dijon mustard

½ tsp lemon juice

½ tsp white vinegar

¼ tsp fine grind sea salt

⅛ tsp ground black pepper

¼ tsp ground turmeric

EGGS BENEDICT BELL PEPPER CUPS

These mildly spicy, flavorful eggs are neatly contained in the bell peppers and served with a creamy and slightly tangy faux hollandaise sauce. These are simple to prepare, done in minutes, and gluten-free.

1 Place the steam rack in the inner pot and add 1 cup water to the bottom of the pot.

2 Make the sauce by combining the mayonnaise, Dijon mustard, lemon juice, vinegar, sea salt, black pepper, and turmeric in a small bowl. Whisk until blended. Cover and refrigerate.

3 Carefully crack 1 egg into each bell pepper cup, making sure to keep the yolk intact, and cover the top of each pepper with a small square of aluminum foil. Place the covered peppers on the steam rack.

4 Cover, lock the lid, and flip the steam release handle to the sealing position. Select **Pressure Cook (High)** and set the cook time for **3 minutes.**

5 When the cook time is complete, allow the pressure to release naturally for 2 minutes and then quick release the remaining pressure.

6 Open the lid and transfer the peppers to a serving platter.

7 Remove the foil and top each pepper with 1 tablespoon of the sauce, and then garnish with the arugula leaves. Serve hot.

tip *For a softer yolk, reduce the pressure time to 2 minutes; for a firmer yolk, increase the pressure time to 4 minutes.*

Nutrition per serving
CALORIES: 200   **FAT:** 15g   **NET CARBS:** 9g   **PROTEIN:** 8g

CREAMY ALMOND FLAX PORRIDGE

This hot and creamy cereal features accents of cinnamon and vanilla, and is topped with sweet, fresh berries. Keto, gluten-free, and paleo-friendly, this satisfying warm porridge is ready in just 4 minutes!

SERVES: 4
SERVING SIZE:
½ CUP PORRIDGE WITH
½ CUP BERRIES

PREP: 2 MINUTES
PRESSURE: 2 MINUTES
TOTAL: 4 MINUTES

SETTING: PORRIDGE
RELEASE: QUICK

1 Add the sunflower seeds to a small food processor or blender. Pulse until a flourlike texture is achieved.

2 In a medium bowl, combine the sunflower meal, almond flour, and flaxseed meal. Mix until well combined.

3 Add the melted butter or ghee to the pot and then add the almond-flaxseed mixture and water. Stir until well combined.

4 Cover, lock the lid, and flip the steam release handle to the sealing position. Select **Porridge (High)** and set the cook time for **2 minutes**

5 When the cook time is complete, quick release the pressure.

6 Open the lid and stir in the almond milk and vanilla extract. (If the porridge is too thick, add more water, 1 tbsp at a time, until the desired consistency is achieved.)

7 Spoon the porridge into serving bowls. Top each serving with ⅛ teaspoon cinnamon, 1 teaspoon sweetener, and ½ cup of the berries. Serve warm.

8 tbsp unsalted and shelled raw sunflower seeds

10 tbsp almond flour

4 tbsp golden flaxseed meal

2½ tbsp butter or ghee, melted

2⅓ cups water

1 cup unsweetened almond milk

½ tsp vanilla extract

½ tsp ground cinnamon

4 tsp erythritol-oligosaccharide granular sweetener blend

2 cups mixed berries (blueberries, raspberries, or blackberries)

tip *To make this recipe dairy-free, substitute 2½ tbsp coconut oil for the butter.*

Nutrition per serving
CALORIES: 310   **FAT:** 27g   **NET CARBS:** 6g   **PROTEIN:** 10g

SLOW COOKER GERMAN PANCAKE

This giant pancake is surprisingly low in carbs compared to traditional pancakes. It has the texture of a thick crepe, is lightly sweet, and is topped with a drizzle of melted butter and a dollop of sugar-free jam.

SERVES: 6
SERVING SIZE: 1 SLICE

PREP: 5 MINUTES
COOK: 1 HOUR 30 MINUTES
TOTAL: 1 HOUR 35 MINUTES

SETTING: SLOW COOK
RELEASE: NONE

1 In a large bowl, combine the eggs, almond milk, lemon juice, and vanilla extract. Whisk to combine. Set aside.

2 In a medium bowl, combine the almond flour, sweetener, baking powder, and sea salt. Mix well.

3 Add the wet ingredients to the dry ingredients and mix until the batter is well combined and no lumps remain.

4 Coat the bottom of the inner pot with 1 tbsp of the melted butter and then add the batter.

5 Cover and lock the lid, but leave the steam release handle in the venting position. Select **Slow Cook (High)**, adjust the mode to **More**, and set the cook time for **1 hour 30 minutes.**

6 When the cook time is complete, open the lid and insert a toothpick into the center of the pancake to check for doneness. (The toothpick should come out clean.)

7 Remove the inner pot from the base. Using a spatula, carefully loosen the edges of the pancake from the sides of the pot and transfer the pancake to a large plate. Use the spatula to flip the pancake over so the browned side is facing up.

8 Slice into 6 equal-sized wedges. Drizzle 1 teaspoon of the melted butter over each wedge and then top each serving with 1 teaspoon of the berry jam. Serve warm.

4 large eggs

½ cup unsweetened almond milk

½ tsp lemon juice

1 tsp vanilla extract

1 cup almond flour

¼ cup erythritol and oligosaccharide-blend granular sweetener

½ tsp baking powder

¼ tsp fine grind sea salt

3 tbsp melted butter, divided

2 tbsp no-sugar-added berry jam

tip *Use a jam that is labeled sugar-free, no-sugar-added, or stevia-sweetened, and look for varieties such as mixed berry, strawberry, blueberry, raspberry, or blackberry.*

Nutrition per serving
CALORIES: 138 **FAT:** 11g **NET CARBS:** 3g **PROTEIN:** 5g

SERVES: 6
SERVING SIZE: 1 MUFFIN

PREP: 6 MINUTES
PRESSURE: 20 MINUTES
TOTAL: 36 MINUTES

SETTING: PRESSURE COOK
RELEASE: NATURAL/QUICK

⅓ cup coconut flour

1½ tbsp golden flaxseed meal

4½ tbsp erythritol and oligosaccharide-blend granular sweetener

1 tsp baking powder

¼ tsp baking soda

⅛ tsp fine grind sea salt

⅓ cup unsweetened almond milk

2 large eggs, beaten

1½ tbsp butter, melted

1 tsp vanilla extract

⅓ cup fresh blueberries

tip *To make this recipe dairy-free, substitute 1½ tbsp coconut oil for the butter.*

LIGHT AND SWEET BLUEBERRY MUFFINS

Low in carbs and bursting with fresh blueberries, these lightly sweet muffins are the perfect accompaniment to your morning coffee or tea. And at only two net carbs, they also are a perfect between-meal snack.

1 In a large bowl, combine the coconut flour, flaxseed meal, sweetener, baking powder, baking soda, and sea salt. Mix until combined and no large lumps remain. Set aside.

2 In a medium bowl, combine the almond milk, eggs, melted butter, and vanilla extract. Mix thoroughly.

3 Add the wet ingredients to the dry ingredients and mix until a smooth consistency is achieved and no lumps remain. Gently fold the blueberries into the batter.

4 Fill six silicone muffin cups three-quarters full with the muffin batter, making sure to evenly divide the blueberries between the cups. Use a spoon to smooth the batter and press the blueberries down into the batter.

5 Add 1 cup water to the bottom of the pot. Place a 10-inch (25cm) sheet of aluminum foil over the steam rack. Place the filled muffin cups on top of the rack and then fold the excess foil up and around the sides of the muffin cups.

6 Grasp the rack handles and lower the rack into the pot. Loosely cover the muffins with an additional 10-inch (25cm) sheet of aluminum foil.

7 Cover, lock the lid, and flip the steam release handle to the sealing position. Select **Pressure Cook (High)** and set the cook time for **20 minutes.**

8 When the cook time is complete, allow the pressure to release naturally for 10 minutes and then quick release the remaining pressure.

9 Open the lid, remove the foil, and carefully grasp the steam rack handles to lift the rack and muffins out of the pot. Remove the muffins from the silicone cups. Serve warm.

Nutrition per serving
CALORIES: 89   **FAT:** 6g   **NET CARBS:** 2g   **PROTEIN:** 3g

CHEESY SPINACH MUSHROOM FRITTATA

This light and fluffy frittata is crust free, low carb, and loaded with protein-rich eggs, healthy spinach, and mushrooms. It's perfect served for breakfast, or even as a light lunch.

 SERVES: 6
SERVING SIZE: 1 SLICE

 PREP: 4 MINUTES
PRESSURE: 30 MINUTES
TOTAL: 50 MINUTES

 SETTING: PRESSURE COOK
RELEASE: NATURAL/QUICK

1 cup sliced fresh mushrooms

1 cup fresh baby spinach leaves

6 large eggs

¼ cup heavy cream

1 tsp fine grind sea salt

½ tsp ground black pepper

½ cup shredded Monterey Jack cheese

½ avocado, sliced

1 Spray a 6.5-inch (16.5cm) 1quart (1l) round soufflé dish with nonstick coconut oil spray. Arrange the mushrooms and spinach leaves in the bottom of the dish. Set aside.

2 In a large bowl, combine the eggs, heavy cream, sea salt, and black pepper. Mix well to combine. Gently pour the egg mixture over the mushrooms and spinach.

3 Add 1½ cups water to the bottom of the inner pot. Place the soufflé dish on the steam rack and grasp the rack handles to lower the rack and dish into the pot.

4 Cover, lock the lid, and flip the steam release handle to the sealing position. Select **Pressure Cook (High)** and set the cook time for **30 minutes.**

5 When the cook time is complete, allow the pressure to release naturally for 10 minutes and then quick release the remaining pressure.

6 Open the lid and sprinkle the Jack cheese over top of the frittata. Replace the lid and allow the residual heat to melt the cheese for 5 minutes.

7 Open the lid and carefully grasp the rack handles to lift the rack and dish out of the pot. Transfer the frittata to a serving platter, cut into 6 equal-sized wedges, and top with the sliced avocado. Serve warm.

tip *To make this recipe dairy-free, substitute ¼ cup unsweetened almond milk for the heavy cream and ½ cup shredded almond cheese for the Jack cheese.*

Nutrition per serving
CALORIES: 170 **FAT:** 13g **NET CARBS:** 2g **PROTEIN:** 10g

SERVES: 2
SERVING SIZE: 1 LATTE

PREP: 2 MINUTES
PRESSURE: 4 MINUTES
TOTAL: 11 MINUTES

SETTING: PRESSURE COOK
RELEASE: NATURAL/QUICK

1⅔ cups unsweetened, unflavored almond milk

½ cup espresso or strongly brewed coffee

¼ cup no-sugar-added pumpkin purée

½ tsp stevia extract

1 tsp pumpkin pie spice

1 tsp vanilla extract

4 tbsp heavy cream

PUMPKIN SPICE LATTE

This sweet and creamy pumpkin latte features warm autumn spices and a light and fluffy whipped cream topping. It's a warm and lovely cold-morning treat that is low in carbs.

1 Combine the almond milk, espresso or coffee, and pumpkin purée in the inner pot.

2 Cover, lock the lid, and flip the steam release handle to the sealing position. Select **Pressure Cook (High)** and set the cook time for **4 minutes.**

3 When the cook time is complete, allow the pressure to release naturally for 5 minutes and then quick release the remaining pressure.

4 Open the lid and add the stevia, pumpkin pie spice, and vanilla extract. Whisk until blended.

5 Add the heavy cream to a tall container and use an immersion blender to whip the cream until stiff peaks are formed.

6 Place a fine-mesh sieve over 2 mugs and fill each with 1¼ cup of the latte, and then top each serving with 2 tablespoons of the whipped cream. Serve hot.

tip *To make this recipe dairy-free, substitute 4 tbsp coconut cream for the heavy cream.*

If you don't have pumpkin pie spice, you can make your own by combining ½ tsp cinnamon, ¼ tsp ground ginger, and ¼ tsp ground nutmeg.

Nutrition per serving
CALORIES: 146   **FAT:** 14g   **NET CARBS:** 3g   **PROTEIN:** 2g

SERVES: 4
SERVING SIZE:
1 EGG WITH ⅓ CUP MEAT SAUCE

PREP: 6 MINUTES
PRESSURE: 0 MINUTES
TOTAL: 20 MINUTES

SETTINGS: SAUTÉ/PRESSURE COOK
RELEASE: QUICK

1 tbsp olive oil

⅓lb (151g) ground beef

¼ cup minced onion

2 garlic cloves, minced

3 tbsp diced red bell pepper

1½ cups no-sugar-added tomato sauce

⅓ cup water

½ tbsp Italian seasoning blend

½ tsp garlic powder

½ tsp fine grind sea salt

¼ tsp ground black pepper

4 large eggs

⅓ cup shredded whole milk mozzarella cheese

1 tbsp chopped flat-leaf parsley

EGGS IN PURGATORY
Italian-Style

These bold and flavorful eggs are big on flavor, high in protein, and smothered in a mouth-watering meat sauce. This zesty and satisfying dish is believed to be a hangover cure in Italy!

1 Select **Sauté (Normal).** Once the pot is hot, add the olive oil and ground beef. Sauté for 4 minutes or until the meat is browned, using a wooden spoon to stir and break up the meat.

2 Add the onion, garlic, and bell pepper to the pot. Sauté for 2–3 additional minutes or until the vegetables are softened.

3 Add the tomato sauce, water, Italian seasoning, garlic powder, sea salt, and black pepper. Stir to combine and then press **Cancel** to turn off the pot. Allow the mixture to cool in the pot for 4 minutes.

4 Carefully crack the eggs into the pot, spacing them evenly over the meat sauce and keeping the yolks intact.

5 Cover, lock the lid, and flip the steam release handle to the sealing position. Select **Pressure Cook (Low)** and set the cook time for **0 minutes.** (The eggs will cook during the pressure building phase of the pressure cook setting.)

6 When the build time is complete, quick release the pressure.

7 Open the lid and sprinkle the mozzarella and parsley over top. Slice into 4 equal-sized portions. Serve hot.

tip *To make this recipe dairy-free, omit the mozzarella.*

Nutrition per serving
CALORIES: 237   **FAT:** 14g   **NET CARBS:** 7g   **PROTEIN:** 31g

SAVORY SAUSAGE AND SOUR CREAM QUICHE

This savory, fluffy quiche is filled with mild chiles and smoky sausage and topped with a layer of sour cream, salsa, and melted cheese. It's crust-free and very low in carbs, but loaded with flavor.

SERVES: 8
SERVING SIZE: 1 SLICE

PREP: 6 MINUTES
PRESSURE: 32 MINUTES
TOTAL: 1 HOUR

SETTING: PRESSURE COOK
RELEASE: NATURAL/QUICK

1 Spray a 6 x 3-inch (15.25 x 7.5cm) 1-quart (1l) soufflé dish with nonstick coconut oil cooking spray. Arrange the sausage in an even layer in the bottom of the dish. Set aside.

2 In a large bowl, combine the eggs, egg whites, 3 tbsp salsa, heavy cream, green chiles, sea salt, and black pepper. Whisk thoroughly.

3 Pour the egg mixture over the sausage. Set aside.

4 Make the sour cream topping by combining the sour cream and remaining salsa in a small bowl. Stir until blended.

5 Working in small amounts, evenly spoon the sour cream mixture over top of the egg mixture. (The sour cream mixture will sink to the bottom, but will rise back to the top during cooking.) Tightly cover the top of the soufflé dish with a sheet of aluminum foil.

6 Pour 1½ cups water into the bottom of the inner pot. Place the soufflé dish on the steam rack, grasp the steam rack handles, and carefully lower the rack and dish into the pot.

7 Cover, lock the lid, and flip the steam release handle to the sealing position. Select **Pressure Cook (High)** and set the cook time for **32 minutes.**

8 When the cook time is complete, allow the pressure to release naturally for 12 minutes and then quick release the remaining pressure.

9 Open the lid and carefully remove the aluminum foil from the dish. Sprinkle the cheddar cheese over top of the quiche, replace the lid, and wait 3 minutes for the residual heat to melt the cheese.

10 Open the lid, grasp the rack handles and carefully lift the rack and dish out of the pot.

11 Allow the quiche to cool for 8–10 minutes before transferring to a serving plate. Slice into 8 equal-sized wedges. Serve warm.

Four 3-inch (7.5cm) fully cooked pork link sausages, chopped

6 large eggs

½ cup 100% liquid egg whites

4½ tbsp mild salsa (green or red), divided

3 tbsp heavy cream

3 tbsp canned mild green chiles

½ tsp fine grind sea salt

¼ tsp ground black pepper

¼ cup full-fat sour cream

½ cup shredded cheddar cheese

tip *100% liquid egg whites are sold in cartons and can be found in the egg section at the grocery store. If you don't have liquid egg whites, you can replace them with the whites from 4 large eggs.*

Nutrition per serving
CALORIES: 238 **FAT:** 19g **NET CARBS:** 3g **PROTEIN:** 13g

SCOTCH EGGS

Satisfying and savory, these eggs are extremely low in carbs and high in healthy fats. This tasty and robust Scottish-style breakfast treat will satiate your hunger and help keep you feeling full all morning.

SERVES: 4
SERVING SIZE: 1 EGG

PREP: 10 MINUTES
PRESSURE: 16 MINUTES
TOTAL: 36 MINUTES

SETTINGS: PRESSURE COOK/ SAUTÉ/PRESSURE COOK
RELEASE: NATURAL/QUICK

4 eggs

1lb (450g) ground spicy Italian pork sausage, formed into 4 equal-sized patties

1½ tbsp olive oil

1 Fill a large bowl halfway with ice water. Set aside.

2 Place the steam rack in the inner pot and add 1 cup water to the bottom of the pot. Place the eggs on the steam rack.

3 Cover, lock the lid, and flip the steam release handle to the sealing position. Select **Pressure Cook (High)** and set the cook time for **6 minutes.**

4 When the cook time is complete, allow the pressure to release naturally for 5 minutes and then quick release the remaining pressure.

5 Open the lid, carefully transfer the eggs to the ice water bath, and allow to cool for 5 minutes. Once cool enough to handle, peel the eggs and transfer to a platter. Set aside.

6 Remove the steam rack from the inner pot. Carefully remove the inner pot from the base, drain, and then return the pot to the base.

7 Place the sausage patties on a flat surface and place 1 egg in the center of each patty. Carefully wrap the sausage around each egg and gently shape until the eggs are covered in the sausage.

8 Select **Sauté (Normal).** Once the pot is hot, add the olive oil. Carefully place the eggs in the pot and brown on all sides for 6 minutes, using tongs to continuously turn the eggs. Once the eggs are browned, transfer to a large plate and press **Cancel** to turn off the pot.

9 Place the steam rack back in the inner pot and add 1 cup water to the bottom of the pot. Carefully place the eggs on the rack.

10 Cover, lock the lid, and flip the steam release handle to the sealing position. Select **Pressure Cook (High)** and set the cook time for **10 minutes.**

11 When the cook time is complete, quick release the pressure and open the lid.

12 Using tongs, carefully transfer the Scotch eggs to a serving platter. Serve warm.

tip *Depending on your taste preferences, you also can use gluten-free, mild, or hot varieties of ground pork sausage.*

Nutrition per serving
CALORIES: 456   **FAT:** 36g   **NET CARBS:** 2g   **PROTEIN:** 25g

SERVES: 2
SERVING SIZE: 1 RAMEKIN

PREP: 5 MINUTES
PRESSURE: 2 MINUTES
TOTAL: 20 MINUTES

SETTINGS: SAUTÉ/PRESSURE COOK
RELEASE: NATURAL/QUICK

2 tbsp butter, divided

⅔ cup grated zucchini

2 slices cooked bacon, chopped

¼ cup shredded cheddar cheese

2 large eggs

¼ tsp fine grind sea salt

¼ tsp ground black pepper

ZUCCHINI BACON HASH
with Eggs

Savory and smoky, this keto-friendly hash features eggs, crisp bacon, and gooey cheddar cheese. To help keep the carbs low, it's made with grated zucchini instead of potatoes.

1 Select **Sauté (Normal)** and add 1 tbsp butter to the inner pot. Once the butter is melted, add the zucchini and sauté for 3 minutes or until the zucchini softens and begins to brown. Press **Cancel** to turn off the pot.

2 Transfer the zucchini to a medium bowl and add the bacon and cheese. Stir to combine. Set aside.

3 Remove the inner pot from the base, rinse and wipe dry, and then return the pot to the base. Place the steam rack in the inner pot and add 1½ cups water to the bottom of the pot.

4 Coat two 3-ounce (85g) ramekins with the remaining butter. Add equal amounts of the zucchini mixture to each ramekin.

5 Crack 1 egg into each ramekin, being careful not to break the yolks. Place the ramekins on the steam rack.

6 Cover, lock the lid, and flip the steam release handle to the sealing position. Select **Pressure Cook (High)** and set the cook time for **2 minutes.**

7 When the cook time is complete, allow the pressure to release naturally for 10 minutes and then quick release the remaining pressure.

8 Open the lid, carefully grasp the steam rack handles, and lift the rack and ramekins out of the pot.

9 Season each serving with the sea salt and black pepper. Serve warm.

tip *Use ovenproof ramekins that are small enough to fit in the inner pot; preferably no smaller than 3 inches (7.5cm) in diameter and no larger than 4 inches (10cm) in diameter.*

Nutrition per serving
CALORIES: 295   **FAT:** 23g   **NET CARBS:** 4g   **PROTEIN:** 14g

STEAMED EGGS EN COCOTTE
with Cheese and Chives

These delicious French-style eggs are delicate, with a subtle blend of flavors. They're simple to make, quick to prepare, and extremely low in carbs with only one net carb per serving.

1 Coat the insides of four 4-inch (10cm) ramekins with the butter.

2 Add ½ tbsp heavy cream to each ramekin. Carefully crack 1 egg into each ramekin and then sprinkle the chives over top of the eggs.

3 Insert the steam rack in the inner pot and add 1 cup water to the bottom of the pot. Place the ramekins on the steam rack.

4 Cover, lock the lid, and flip the steam release handle to the sealing position. Select **Pressure Cook (Low)** and set the cook time for **2 minutes**.

5 When the cook time is complete, quick release the pressure.

6 Open the lid, carefully grasp the steam rack handles, and lift the rack and ramekins out of the pot.

7 Sprinkle equal amounts of the feta over top of each ramekin and then season each serving with the sea salt and black pepper. Serve warm.

SERVES: 4
SERVING SIZE: 1 RAMEKIN

PREP: 1 MINUTE
PRESSURE: 2 MINUTES
TOTAL: 3 MINUTES

SETTING: PRESSURE COOK
RELEASE: QUICK

2 tbsp butter
2 tbsp heavy cream
4 large eggs
1 tbsp chopped chives
2 tbsp crumbled feta cheese
¼ tsp fine grind sea salt
⅛ tsp ground black pepper

tip *Use ovenproof ramekins that are small enough to fit in the inner pot; preferably no smaller than 3 inches (7.5cm) in diameter and no larger than 4 inches (10cm) in diameter.*

Nutrition per serving
CALORIES: 160 **FAT:** 14g **NET CARBS:** 1g **PROTEIN:** 7g

DINNERS, SOUPS, AND STEWS

SERVES: 4
SERVING SIZE: ⅔ CUP SHRIMP WITH SAUCE WITH 1 CUP CAULIFLOWER RICE

PREP: 6 MINUTES
PRESSURE: 2 MINUTES
TOTAL: 13 MINUTES

SETTINGS: PRESSURE COOK/SAUTÉ/MEAT STEW
RELEASE: NATURAL/QUICK

1 medium head cauliflower, trimmed, stem removed, and cut into medium-sized florets

2 tbsp olive oil

3 tbsp butter

5 garlic cloves, minced

⅓ cup white wine or cooking wine

1 cup chicken broth

2lbs (1kg) uncooked shrimp, peeled and deveined

1½ tbsp fresh lemon juice

1 tsp fine grind sea salt

½ tsp ground black pepper

1 tbsp chopped fresh parsley

tip *If you don't have a steamer basket with legs, you can use an ovenproof bowl placed on top of the steam rack.*

GARLIC SHRIMP SCAMPI
with Cauliflower Rice

This buttery shrimp is accented with fragrant garlic and touches of lemon and white wine, and is served over low-carb cauliflower rice. It's a keto version of a classic dish that is simple to prepare.

1 Place a steamer basket with legs in the inner pot and add 1 cup water to the bottom of the pot. Add the cauliflower to the steamer basket.

2 Cover, lock the lid, and flip the steam release handle to the sealing position. Select **Pressure Cook (High)** and set the cook time for **1 minute.**

3 When the cook time is complete, quick release the pressure.

4 Open the lid and carefully remove the steamer basket and cauliflower from the inner pot. Set aside.

5 Carefully remove the inner pot from the base, drain and wipe dry with a paper towel, and return the pot to the base.

6 Add the cauliflower florets to a food processor or blender and pulse until a ricelike texture is formed. Set aside.

7 Select **Sauté (Normal).** Add the olive oil and butter to the inner pot. Once the butter is melted, add the garlic and sauté for 3 minutes or until the garlic becomes fragrant.

8 Add the wine and chicken broth to the pot and simmer for 2 minutes, using a wooden spoon to stir the ingredients and scrape any browned bits from the bottom of the pot. Press **Cancel** to turn off the pot. Add the shrimp and stir.

9 Cover, lock the lid, and flip the steam release handle to the sealing position. Select **Meat Stew (High)** and set the cook time for **1 minute.**

10 When the cook time is complete, allow the pressure to release naturally for 5 minutes and then quick release the remaining pressure.

11 Open the lid. Add the lemon juice, sea salt, and black pepper. Stir.

12 Transfer the cauliflower rice to a serving platter. Ladle the shrimp and sauce over the rice and garnish with the parsley. Serve warm.

Nutrition per serving
CALORIES: 361   **FAT:** 18g   **NET CARBS:** 7g   **PROTEIN:** 32g

SERVES: 4
SERVING SIZE: 1 PEPPER

PREP: 5 MINUTES
PRESSURE: 15 MINUTES
TOTAL: 50 MINUTES

SETTINGS: PRESSURE COOK/
STAY WARM
RELEASE: NATURAL/QUICK

4 medium bell peppers, tops and seeds removed

1lb (450g) ground pork sausage

1 large egg

2 garlic cloves, minced

3 tbsp tomato paste

½ tsp fine grind sea salt

¼ tsp ground black pepper

½ tbsp Italian seasoning blend

½ tsp onion powder

⅓ cup no-sugar-added tomato sauce

4 slices mozzarella cheese

ITALIAN-STYLE STUFFED BELL PEPPERS

These warm and smoky bell peppers are filled with savory meat, spices, and a rich marinara sauce and then topped with melted cheese. This hearty Italian-style dish is made in a snap in the Instant Pot.

1 Using a fork, pierce small holes into the bottoms of the peppers to allow excess fat from the meat to drain. Set aside.

2 In a large mixing bowl, combine the sausage, egg, garlic, tomato paste, sea salt, black pepper, Italian seasoning, and onion powder. Mix thoroughly to combine.

3 Stuff each bell pepper with the meat mixture, filling each pepper nearly to the top.

4 Place the steam rack in the inner pot and add 1 cup water. Place the stuffed peppers bottom-side-down on the rack. Pour the tomato sauce over top of each pepper.

5 Cover, lock the lid, and flip the steam release handle to the sealing position. Select **Pressure Cook (High)** and set the cook time for **15 minutes.**

6 When the cook time is complete, allow the pressure to release naturally for 5 minutes and then quick release the remaining pressure.

7 Open the lid and top each pepper with 1 slice of the mozzarella. Replace the lid, select **Stay Warm,** and set the cook time for **2 minutes** to melt the cheese.

8 Open the lid and use tongs to carefully transfer the peppers to a large serving platter. Serve warm.

tip *To make this recipe dairy-free, substitute 4 slices almond cheese for the mozzarella or just omit the cheese.*

Nutrition per serving
CALORIES: 369   **FAT:** 22g   **NET CARBS:** 8g   **PROTEIN:** 17g

CORNED BEEF AND CABBAGE

This traditional Irish favorite is virtually carb free and simple to prepare in the Instant Pot. It features a savory, spiced corned beef brisket that's served with tender cabbage and vegetables.

SERVES: 8
SERVING SIZE: ⅓LB (151G) BRISKET WITH ⅓ CUP CABBAGE

PREP: 5 MINUTES
PRESSURE: 1 HOUR 2 MINUTES
TOTAL: 1 HOUR 45 MINUTES

SETTINGS: MEAT STEW/SOUP
RELEASE: NATURAL/QUICK

1 Add the brisket to the inner pot. Add 4 cups water to the pot, or just enough water to cover the brisket. Add the garlic, mustard seed, and black peppercorns.

2 Cover, lock the lid, and flip the steam release handle to the sealing position. Select **Meat Stew (High)** and set the cook time for **50 minutes.**

3 While the brisket is cooking, preheat the oven to 170°F (77°C). Place a large ovenproof serving platter in the oven to warm for 8 minutes.

4 When the cook time is complete, allow the pressure to release naturally (about 20 minutes). Open the lid and transfer only the brisket to the warmed platter.

5 Add the onion, celery, and cabbage to the pot.

6 Cover, lock the lid, and flip the steam release handle to the sealing position. Select **Soup (High)** and set the cook time for **12 minutes.**

7 When the cook time is complete, quick release the pressure. Open the lid, add the brisket back to the pot and let warm in the pot for 5 minutes.

8 Transfer the warmed brisket back to the platter and thinly slice. Use a slotted spoon to transfer the vegetables to the platter. Serve hot.

3lbs (1.36kg) corned beef brisket
3 garlic cloves, minced
2 tsp yellow mustard seed
2 tsp black peppercorns
½ large white onion, chopped
3 celery stalks, chopped
1 green cabbage, cut into quarters

tip *Always discard the spice packet that comes with the brisket. Some spice packets contain chemicals, so it's always best to use natural spices.*

Nutrition per serving
CALORIES: 332   **FAT:** 21g   **NET CARBS:** 0g   **PROTEIN:** 23g

GREEK CHICKEN AND VEGETABLE POT

Succulent chicken and vegetables are cooked in an enticing simmer sauce in this classic, colorful, Mediterranean-inspired dish that features piquant flavors and aromatic Greek-inspired spices.

SERVES: 4
SERVING SIZE: 1 CHICKEN THIGH WITH ½ CUP VEGETABLES IN SAUCE

PREP: 5 MINUTES
PRESSURE: 13 MINUTES
TOTAL: 32 MINUTES

SETTINGS: SAUTÉ/PRESSURE COOK
RELEASE: NATURAL/QUICK

1 In a medium bowl, combine the chicken broth, lemon juice, vinegar, thyme, and oregano. Mix well. Set aside.

2 Select **Sauté (Normal).** Once the pot is hot, add the olive oil and garlic and sauté for 1 minute.

3 Season both sides of the chicken thighs with the salt and pepper. Add the chicken thighs to the pot and sauté for 2 minutes per side or until browned.

4 Top the chicken thighs with the artichokes, olives, and diced tomatoes. Sprinkle the pancetta over the chicken and pour the chicken broth mixture into the pot.

5 Cover, lock the lid, and flip the steam release handle to the sealing position. Select **Pressure Cook (High)** and set the cook time for **13 minutes.**

6 Once the cook time is complete, allow the pressure to release naturally for 10 minutes and then quick release the remaining pressure.

7 Open the lid and transfer the chicken to a serving platter. Sprinkle the feta over top. Serve warm.

2 cups chicken broth

1½ tbsp lemon juice

2 tbsp red wine vinegar

1 tsp dried thyme

½ tsp dried oregano

2 tbsp olive oil

3 garlic cloves, minced

1½ lbs (680g) bone-in, skin-on chicken thighs

½ tsp fine grind sea salt

¼ tsp ground black pepper

1⅓ cups canned artichoke quarters, drained

1 cup pitted green olives

⅓ cup diced tomatoes

¼ cup diced pancetta

⅓ cup crumbled feta cheese

tip *If using boneless, skinless chicken thighs, reduce the cooking time to 8 minutes.*

To make this recipe dairy-free, omit the feta.

Nutrition per serving
CALORIES: 420   **FAT:** 23g   **NET CARBS:** 8g   **PROTEIN:** 39g

SERVES: 6
SERVING SIZE: 1 SLICE

PREP: 6 MINUTES
PRESSURE: 20 MINUTES
TOTAL: 38 MINUTES

SETTINGS: SAUTÉ/PRESSURE COOK
RELEASE: NATURAL/QUICK

1 tbsp olive oil

1lb (450g) ground beef

½ cup no-sugar-added tomato sauce

1 garlic clove, minced

2 tbsp golden flaxseed meal

3 eggs (1 beaten)

½ tsp Italian seasoning blend

½ tsp fine grind sea salt

½ tsp smoked paprika

½ tsp onion powder

2 tbsp heavy cream

½ tsp ground mustard

¼ tsp ground black pepper

½ cup grated cheddar cheese

tip *To make this recipe dairy-free, substitute 2 tbsp unsweetened, unflavored almond milk for the heavy cream and ½ cup grated almond cheese for the cheddar.*

CHEESEBURGER PIE

Hearty and comforting, this satisfying keto meat pie is big on taste, but low on carbs. This savory, crust-free pie is made keto friendly by using high-fiber flaxseed meal instead of breadcrumbs.

1 Coat a 6 x 3-inch (15.25 x 7.5cm) round cake pan with the olive oil.

2 Select **Sauté (Normal)**. Once the pot is hot, add the ground beef and sauté for 5 minutes or until the beef is browned. Press **Cancel** to turn off the pot.

3 Carefully remove the inner pot from the base and drain the excess fat from the pot. Transfer the drained beef to a large bowl.

4 Add the tomato sauce, garlic, flaxseed meal, 1 beaten egg, Italian seasoning, sea salt, smoked paprika, and onion powder to the bowl. Mix until well combined.

5 Transfer the meat mixture to the prepared cake pan and use a knife to spread the mixture into an even layer. Set aside.

6 In a separate medium bowl, combine the 2 remaining eggs, heavy cream, ground mustard, and black pepper. Whisk until combined.

7 Pour the egg mixture over the meat mixture. Tightly cover the pan with a sheet of aluminum foil.

8 Place the steam rack in the inner pot and add 2 cups water to the bottom of the pot. Place the pan on the steam rack.

9 Cover, lock the lid, and flip the steam release handle to the sealing position. Select **Pressure Cook (High)** and set the cook time for **20 minutes.**

10 When the cook time is complete, allow the pressure to release naturally for 10 minutes and then quick release the remaining pressure. Press **Cancel** to turn off the pot and allow the pie to rest in the pot for 5 minutes.

11 While the pie is resting, preheat the oven broiler to 450°F (232°C).

12 Open the lid, grasp the rack handles, and carefully lift the rack and pan out of the pot. Remove the foil and sprinkle the cheddar over top of the pie.

13 Place the pie in the oven and broil for 1–2 minutes or until the cheese is melted and the top becomes golden brown. Slice into six equal-sized wedges. Serve hot.

Nutrition per serving
CALORIES: 250   **FAT:** 18g   **NET CARBS:** 2g   **PROTEIN:** 22g

SLOW COOKER PIZZA CASSEROLE

This casserole features the heavenly taste of pepperoni pizza! It's crust-free and has all the satisfying pizza flavors you've been craving, but without all the heavy carbs!

SERVES: 6
SERVING SIZE: 1 SLICE

PREP: 10 MINUTES
COOK: 3 HOURS
TOTAL: 3 HOURS 20 MINUTES

SETTING: SLOW COOK
RELEASE: NONE

1 Select **Sauté (Normal).** Once the pot is hot, add 1 tbsp olive oil and crumble the ground beef into the pot. Sauté for 4 minutes, stirring constantly, until the meat is browned. Press **Cancel** to turn off heat.

2 Place a colander over a large bowl. Transfer the meat to the colander to drain and then transfer the drained meat to a large mixing bowl. Return the inner pot to base.

3 To the bowl with the meat, add 1 cup mozzarella, ½ tablespoon Italian seasoning, and ½ tsp garlic powder. Mix until well combined. Set aside.

4 In a small bowl, combine the tomato sauce, remaining Italian seasoning, remaining garlic powder, oregano, and sea salt. Mix well. Set aside.

5 Coat the bottom of the inner pot with the remaining olive oil. Press the meat mixture into an even layer in the bottom of the pot.

6 Add the tomato sauce mixture to the pot and use a spoon to evenly distribute the sauce over the meat. Add the pepperoni in an even layer over the sauce. Sprinkle the remaining mozzarella over top and then top with the olives.

7 Cover and lock the lid, but leave the steam release handle in the venting position. Select **Slow Cook (Normal)** and set the cook time for **3 hours.**

8 When the cook time is complete, open the lid and transfer the casserole to a serving platter. Slice into six equal-sized wedges. Serve hot.

2 tbsp olive oil, divided

1lb (450g) ground beef

2 cups shredded whole mozzarella cheese, divided

1 tbsp Italian seasoning blend, divided

1 tsp garlic powder, divided

½ cup no-sugar-added tomato sauce

¼ tsp dried oregano

¼ tsp fine grind sea salt

15 slices pepperoni

2 tbsp sliced black olives

tip *To make this recipe dairy-free, substitute 2 cups shredded almond cheese for the mozzarella.*

Nutrition per serving
CALORIES: 320   **FAT:** 23g   **NET CARBS:** 3g   **PROTEIN:** 25g

SERVES: 4
SERVING SIZE:
¼LB (115G) STEAK

PREP: 5 MINUTES
PRESSURE: 25 MINUTES
TOTAL: 45 MINUTES

SETTINGS: SAUTÉ/PRESSURE COOK
RELEASE: NATURAL/QUICK

⅓ cup chopped flat-leaf parsley

3 large garlic cloves, minced

½ tsp dried oregano

¼ tsp crushed red pepper

1 tsp fine grind sea salt, divided

1 tsp ground black pepper, divided

2½ tbsp red wine vinegar

1 tsp lemon juice

½ cup extra virgin olive oil

1lb (450g) skirt steak, trimmed and cut into 4 equal-sized pieces

1 tbsp avocado oil

tip *Alternatively, you can use a foil-covered 6-inch (15.25cm) souffle dish in place of a foil packet.*

ZESTY CHIMICHURRI SKIRT STEAK

This Argentinian-inspired steak is tender and juicy, and features a zesty and refreshingly tangy sauce. It's low in carbs and bursting with flavor, and also gluten-free, dairy-free, and paleo-friendly.

1 Make the chimichurri sauce by adding the parsley to a blender or food processor and pulsing until finely chopped. Add the garlic, oregano, crushed red pepper, ½ tsp sea salt, ½ tsp black pepper, red wine vinegar, and lemon juice. Pulse until combined. Add the olive oil and pulse until the ingredients are well blended. Set aside.

2 Season both sides of the steaks with the remaining salt and pepper.

3 Select **Sauté (Normal).** Once the inner pot is hot, add the avocado oil and let heat for 1 minute. Add the steaks to the pot, two at a time, and sauté for 1–2 minutes per side or until browned on both sides. Transfer the browned steaks to a plate and repeat with the remaining steaks.

4 Cut two 25-inch (63.5cm) sheets of aluminum foil and place one sheet on a flat surface. Place two steaks in the center of the sheet and pour half the chimichurri sauce over top of the steaks. Place the remaining steaks on top and pour the remaining sauce over top.

5 Place the second sheet of foil over the steaks and tightly roll and crimp the ends to create a foil packet. (Make sure the packet is wrapped tightly enough that it will fit in the inner pot.)

6 Place the steam rack in the pot and add 1 cup water to the bottom of the pot. Place the foil packet on top of the rack.

7 Cover, lock the lid, and flip the steam release handle to the sealing position. Select **Pressure Cook (High)** and set the cook time for **25 minutes.**

8 When the cook time is complete, allow the pressure to release naturally for 6 minutes and then quick release the remaining pressure.

9 Open the lid, carefully grasp the rack handles and lift the steam rack and steaks out of the pot. Set the steaks aside to rest for 2 minutes.

10 Open the packet and transfer the steaks to a cutting board. Thinly slice and transfer to a serving platter. Serve warm.

Nutrition per serving
CALORIES: 445   **FAT:** 30g   **NET CARBS:** 2g   **PROTEIN:** 30g

SERVES: 6
SERVING SIZE: ½LB (225G) ROAST WITH ¼ CUP BROTH

PREP: 6 MINUTES
PRESSURE: 1 HOUR
TOTAL: 1 HOUR 35 MINUTES

SETTINGS: SAUTÉ/PRESSURE COOK
RELEASE: NATURAL/QUICK

1½ cups beef broth

¼ cup red cooking wine

1 tbsp dried thyme

½ tbsp dried rosemary

1½ tsp fine grind sea salt

1 tsp paprika

1 tsp garlic powder

½ tsp ground black pepper

3lbs (1.4kg) boneless chuck roast

1½ tbsp avocado oil

2 tbsp unsalted butter

½ medium yellow onion, chopped

2 garlic cloves, minced

1 cup sliced mushrooms

4 stalks celery, chopped

2 sprigs fresh thyme

1 bay leaf

tip *The cook time in this recipe is based on a 3lb (1.4kg) roast. If using a different size roast, adjust the cook time 15 minutes for every pound of roast.*

OLD-FASHIONED POT ROAST

This comforting, juicy pot roast features warm spices and is cooked to tender perfection in a rich beef broth. This keto take on traditional pot roast is gluten-free and extremely low in carbs.

1 In a medium bowl, combine the beef broth, wine, dried thyme, and dried rosemary. Stir to combine. Set aside.

2 In a small bowl, combine the sea salt, paprika, garlic powder, and black pepper. Mix well. Generously rub the dry spice mixture into the roast. Set aside.

3 Select **Sauté (More)**. Once the pot becomes hot, add the avocado oil and butter and heat until the butter is melted, about 2 minutes.

4 Add the roast to the pot. Sauté for 3 minutes per side or until a crust is formed. Transfer the browned roast to a plate and set aside.

5 Add the onions and garlic to the pot. Sauté for 2–3 minutes or until the onions soften and the garlic becomes fragrant.

6 Add half the broth and wine mixture to the pot. Use a wooden spoon to stir and loosen any browned bits from the bottom of the pot.

7 Place the steam rack in the inner pot and place the roast on top of the rack. Add the mushrooms and celery to the pot, and pour the remaining broth and wine mixture over the roast. Place the thyme sprigs and bay leaf on top of the roast.

8 Cover, lock the lid, and flip the steam release handle to the sealing position. Select **Pressure Cook (High)** and set the cook time for **1 hour.** When the cook time is complete, allow the pressure to release naturally for 10 minutes and then quick release the remaining pressure.

9 Open the lid, remove and discard the bay leaf and thyme sprigs, and carefully grasp the steam rack handles to lift the rack and roast out of the pot. Transfer the roast to a serving platter.

10 Transfer the vegetables to the platter and spoon the remaining broth over the roast and vegetables.

11 Slice the roast and ladle ¼ cup of the broth over each serving. Serve hot.

Nutrition per serving
CALORIES: 325   **FAT:** 14g   **NET CARBS:** 3g   **PROTEIN:** 40g

BACON CHEESEBURGER AND RICE CASSEROLE

This savory and hearty bacon cheeseburger casserole is made keto-friendly by using low-carb cauliflower rice in place of traditional rice, which is very high in carbs.

SERVES: 5
SERVING SIZE: 1 SLICE

PREP: 5 MINUTES
PRESSURE: 20 MINUTES
TOTAL: 38 MINUTES

SETTINGS: SAUTÉ/PRESSURE COOK
RELEASE: QUICK

1 Spray a 6.5-inch (16.5cm) 1 quart (1l) round soufflé dish with coconut oil cooking spray. Set aside.

2 Add the cauliflower florets to a food processor and pulse until a ricelike consistency is achieved. Set aside.

3 Select **Sauté (Normal)**. Once the pot is hot, crumble the ground beef into the pot and add the bacon. Sauté for 6 minutes or until the ground beef is thoroughly browned and the bacon is cooked through. Press **Cancel** to turn off the pot. Transfer the beef, bacon, and rendered fat to a large bowl.

4 Carefully remove the inner pot from the base, rinse and wipe dry with a paper towel, and return the pot to the base.

5 Add the tomato sauce, cauliflower rice, garlic powder, paprika, sea salt, black pepper, ½ cup cheddar cheese, and celery seed to the bowl with the beef and bacon. Mix well to combine.

6 Add the mixture to the prepared dish and use a spoon to press and smooth the mixture into an even layer.

7 Place the steam rack in the inner pot and add 1 cup water to the bottom of the pot. Place the dish on top of the rack.

8 Cover, lock the lid, and flip the steam release handle to the sealing position. Select **Pressure Cook (High)** and set the cook time for **20 minutes.** When the cook time is complete, quick release the pressure.

9 Open the lid. Arrange the tomato slices in a single layer on top of the casserole and sprinkle the remaining cheese over top. Replace the lid and let the residual heat melt the cheese for 4–5 minutes.

10 Open the lid, carefully grasp the rack handles, and lift the steam rack and dish out of the pot.

11 Transfer the casserole to a serving plate and slice into 5 equal-sized wedges. Serve warm.

2 cups fresh cauliflower florets

1lb (450g) ground beef

5 slices uncooked bacon, chopped

8oz (225g) no-sugar-added tomato sauce

1 tsp garlic powder

½ tsp paprika

½ tsp fine grind sea salt

¼ tsp ground black pepper

1 cup shredded cheddar cheese, divided

¼ tsp celery seed

1 medium Roma tomato, sliced

tip *To make this recipe dairy-free, substitute 1 cup shredded almond cheese for the cheddar cheese.*

Nutrition per serving
CALORIES: 281   **FAT:** 18g   **NET CARBS:** 4g   **PROTEIN:** 26g

SPAGHETTI SQUASH
with Meat Sauce

Spaghetti squash makes for a lovely pasta alternative in this hearty, keto-friendly version of an Italian classic. Spaghetti squash is low in carbs and so simple to roast whole in the Instant Pot.

1 Select **Sauté (Normal).** Once the pot is hot, add the olive oil, ground beef, garlic, and onions. Sauté, stirring continuously, for about 5 minutes or until the meat is browned.

2 Add the crushed tomatoes, pepperoni or salami, Italian seasoning, garlic powder, parsley, sea salt, black pepper, and beef broth to the pot. Using a wooden spoon, stir and scrape the bottom of the pot to loosen any browned bits. Add the bay leaf.

3 Using a paring knife, pierce the spaghetti squash 4 or 5 times on each side to create holes for venting the steam. Place the squash in the pot and on top of the sauce.

4 Cover, lock the lid, and flip the steam release handle to the sealing position. Select **Pressure Cook (High)** and set the cook time for **18 minutes.** When the cook time is complete, allow the pressure to release naturally for 20 minutes and then quick release the remaining pressure.

5 Open the lid. Using a slotted spoon, carefully transfer the squash to a cutting board and set aside to cool.

6 Add the tomato paste to the pot and stir. Select **Sauté (Less),** replace the lid, and let the sauce simmer for 6 minutes.

7 While the sauce is simmering, slice the cooled squash in half and use a spoon to scoop out the seeds. Using a fork, scrape the flesh to create the noodles.

8 Transfer the noodles to a colander to drain, pressing down on the noodles with paper towels to expel any excess moisture. Transfer the noodles to a serving platter.

9 Remove and discard the bay leaf. Ladle the sauce over top of the noodles and garnish with the Parmesan and basil ribbons (if using). Serve warm.

SERVES: 6
SERVING SIZE:
⅔ CUP SPAGHETTI SQUASH WITH ⅔ CUP MEAT SAUCE

PREP: 5 MINUTES
PRESSURE: 18 MINUTES
TOTAL: 50 MINUTES

SETTINGS: SAUTÉ/
PRESSURE COOK/SAUTÉ
RELEASE: NATURAL/QUICK

1 tbsp olive oil

1lb (450g) ground beef

2 cloves garlic, minced

¼ cup finely chopped yellow onion

28oz (800g) can crushed tomatoes

6 slices uncured pepperoni or salami, chopped

1½ tbsp Italian seasoning blend

1 tsp garlic powder

½ tsp dried parsley

½ tsp fine grind sea salt

½ tsp ground black pepper

⅓ cup beef broth

1 bay leaf

3lb (1.4kg) spaghetti squash, washed and dried

2 tbsp tomato paste

1½ tbsp grated Parmesan cheese

1 tbsp fresh basil ribbons (optional)

tip *Unused portions of the squash noodles and meat sauce can be stored separately in resealable containers in the refrigerator for up to one week.*

Nutrition per serving
CALORIES: 230   **FAT:** 12g   **NET CARBS:** 9g   **PROTEIN:** 19g

SERVES: 4
SERVING SIZE: 2 SLICES

PREP: 8 MINUTES
PRESSURE: 30 MINUTES
TOTAL: 45 MINUTES

SETTING: PRESSURE COOK
RELEASE: QUICK

1lb (450g) ground beef

½ cup no-sugar-added tomato sauce

1 large egg, beaten

2 tbsp golden flaxseed meal

1 tsp garlic powder

1 tsp fine grind sea salt

½ tsp paprika

¼ tsp ground black pepper

4 slices uncooked bacon

⅓ cup shredded cheddar cheese

FOR THE GLAZE

⅓ cup no-sugar-added tomato sauce

2 tsp granular erythritol blend sweetener

1 tsp apple cider vinegar

¼ tsp onion powder

¼ tsp garlic powder

⅛ tsp fine grind sea salt

⅛ tsp allspice

tip *You can use the tomato glaze as a keto-friendly substitute for ketchup.*

BACON CHEDDAR STUFFED MEATLOAF

This comforting meatloaf is full of flavorful spices, filled with smoky bacon and melted cheddar, and topped with a sweet and savory tomato glaze. You'll never believe this recipe is keto!

1 In a large bowl, combine the ground beef, tomato sauce, egg, flaxseed meal, garlic powder, sea salt, paprika, and black pepper. Use your hands to mix until the ingredients are just combined.

2 Place a 20-inch (50cm) sheet of aluminum foil on a flat surface. Place half of the meat mixture in the center of the foil sheet and use your hands to mold the mixture into a flat oval shape that is about 6 inches (15.25cm) long.

3 Place the bacon slices in a single layer on top of the meat and sprinkle the cheddar over top. Place the remaining meat mixture on top and use your hands to shape the mixture into an oval-shaped loaf.

4 Fold the sides of the foil up and around the sides of the meatloaf to form a loaf pan. Set aside.

5 Make the tomato glaze by combining the tomato sauce, sweetener, vinegar, onion powder, garlic powder, sea salt, and allspice in a small bowl. Mix well. Spoon the glaze over the meatloaf.

6 Add 1 cup water to the bottom of the inner pot. Place the loaf on the steam rack and lower the rack into the pot.

7 Cover, lock the lid, and flip the steam release handle to the sealing position. Select **Pressure Cook (High)** and set the cook time for **30 minutes.**

8 While the meatloaf is cooking, preheat the oven broiler to 550°F (288°C).

9 When the cook time for the meatloaf is complete, quick release the pressure, open the lid, and carefully grasp the rack handles to lift the rack and meatloaf out of the pot.

10 Transfer the loaf pan to a large baking sheet. Place the meatloaf under the broiler to brown for 2 minutes or until the glaze is bubbling.

11 Transfer the browned meatloaf to a serving plate, discard the foil, and cut the loaf into 8 equal-sized slices. Serve hot.

Nutrition per serving
CALORIES: 330　**FAT:** 21g　**NET CARBS:** 4g　**PROTEIN:** 31g

CHICKEN ARTICHOKE LEMON PICCATA

Tender chicken and artichokes are served in a refreshing lemon citrus sauce with capers and spices in this keto version of a classic Italian dish that is low in carbs and gluten-free.

SERVES: 4
SERVING SIZE: ½LB (225G) CHICKEN WITH ¼ CUP VEGETABLES AND BROTH

PREP: 4 MINUTES
PRESSURE: 10 MINUTES
TOTAL: 36 MINUTES

SETTINGS: SAUTÉ/PRESSURE COOK
RELEASE: NATURAL/QUICK

1 Season the chicken breasts with the sea salt and black pepper.

2 Select **Sauté (Normal)** and add the butter to the pot. Once the butter is melted, add the chicken breasts and sear for 4 minutes per side or until browned.

3 Add the chicken broth, lemon juice, garlic, artichoke hearts, capers, Italian seasoning, and wine to the pot.

4 Cover, lock the lid, and flip the steam release handle to the sealing position. Select **Pressure Cook (High)** and set the cook time for **10 minutes.**

5 When the cook time is complete, allow the pressure to release naturally for 10 minutes and then quick release the remaining pressure.

6 Open the lid. Transfer the chicken to serving plates and pour ¼ cup of the artichoke mixture and broth over the chicken. Serve hot.

1½lbs (680g) boneless, skinless chicken breasts

½ tsp fine grind sea salt

¼ tsp ground black pepper

2 tbsp butter

⅔ cup chicken broth

2 tbsp fresh lemon juice

4 garlic cloves, minced

1½ cups canned artichoke hearts, drained and quartered

2 tbsp capers

½ tsp Italian seasoning blend

¼ cup white cooking wine

tip *To make this recipe dairy-free, substitute 2 tbsp avocado oil for the butter.*

Nutrition per serving
CALORIES: 275   **FAT:** 8g   **NET CARBS:** 5g   **PROTEIN:** 40g

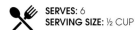

SERVES: 6
SERVING SIZE: ½ CUP

PREP: 10 MINUTES
PRESSURE: 55 MINUTES
TOTAL: 75 MINUTES

SETTINGS: SAUTÉ/PRESSURE COOK
RELEASE: NATURAL/QUICK

2lbs (1kg) pork shoulder, cut into 6 equal-sized pieces

1 tsp fine grind sea salt

½ tsp ground black pepper

2 jalapeño peppers, seeded and stemmed

1lb (450g) tomatillos, husks removed and quartered

3 garlic cloves

1 medium white onion, chopped

1 tsp ground cumin

½ tsp dried oregano

1 tbsp lime juice

3 tbsp fresh cilantro, chopped

1⅔ cups chicken broth

1½ tbsp olive oil

CHILE VERDE PULLED PORK

This tender and juicy pork is cooked in a tomatillo sauce that is bursting with spicy and sweet citrus flavors. The Instant Pot cooks this Mexican favorite fast, while still retaining the slow cooked flavor.

1 Season the pork cuts with the salt and pepper. Gently rub the seasonings into the pork cuts. Set aside.

2 Combine the jalapeños, tomatillos, garlic cloves, onions, cumin, oregano, lime juice, cilantro, and chicken broth in a blender. Pulse until ingredients are well combined. Set aside.

3 Select **Sauté (Normal)** and add the olive oil to the pot. Once the oil is hot, add the pork cuts and sear for 3–4 minutes per side or until browned.

4 Pour the simmer sauce over the pork and lightly stir to coat the cuts in the sauce.

5 Cover, lock the lid, and flip the steam release handle to the sealing position. Select **Pressure Cook (High)** and set the cook time for **55 minutes.**

6 When the cook time is complete, allow the pressure to release naturally for 10 minutes and then quick release the remaining pressure.

7 Open the lid. Transfer the pork cuts to a cutting board and use two forks to shred the pork.

8 Transfer the shredded pork back to the pot and stir to combine the pork with the sauce. Transfer to a serving platter. Serve warm.

tip This is wonderful served over cauliflower rice or in romaine lettuce shells for keto-style tacos.

Nutrition per serving
CALORIES: 342   **FAT:** 23g   **NET CARBS:** 4g   **PROTEIN:** 33g

LEMON DILL SALMON
with Broccoli

Delicate salmon, which is is naturally very low in carbs and high in healthy fats, is topped with a refreshing lemon herb butter and served with tender broccoli in this satisfying one pot meal.

SERVES: 4
SERVING SIZE: ¼LB (115G) SALMON AND ½ CUP BROCCOLI

PREP: 5 MINUTES
PRESSURE: 7 MINUTES
TOTAL: 20 MINUTES

SETTINGS: STEAM/STEAM
RELEASE: QUICK

1 cup water

1 garlic clove, coarsely chopped

4 sprigs fresh dill

1lb (450g) wild-caught salmon, cut into 4 equal-sized fillets

½ tsp fine grind sea salt

¼ tsp ground black pepper

½ tsp garlic powder

2 tbsp butter, divided

½ medium lemon, thinly sliced

¼ tsp dried dill

2 cups fresh broccoli florets

1 Place the steam rack in the inner pot. Add the water, garlic, and dill sprigs to the bottom of the pot.

2 Place the salmon fillets skin-side down on the steam rack. Season the fillets with the sea salt, black pepper, and garlic powder and top each with ½ tbsp butter and 1 lemon slice. Sprinkle the dried dill over top.

3 Cover, lock the lid, and flip the steam release handle to the sealing position. Select **Steam (High)** and set the cook time for **5 minutes.** When the cook time is complete, quick release the pressure.

4 Open the lid, carefully grasp the steam rack handles, and lift the rack and salmon fillets out of the pot. Transfer the fillets to a serving plate. Set aside.

5 Carefully remove the inner pot from the base, drain and wipe dry with a paper towel, and return the pot to the base.

6 Place a steamer basket with legs in the inner pot and add 1 cup water to the bottom of the pot. Add the broccoli florets to the steamer basket.

7 Cover, lock the lid, and flip the steam release handle to the sealing position. Select **Steam (High)** and set the cook time for **2 minutes.** When the cook time is complete, quick release the pressure and open the lid.

8 Using a slotted spoon, transfer the broccoli to the plate with the salmon. Serve warm.

tip *The cook time for this recipe is for an approximate 1-inch-thick (2.5cm) fillet. For a thicker fillet add 2 minutes to the cook time, for a thinner fillet reduce the cook time by 1 minute.*

Nutrition per serving
CALORIES: 280 **FAT:** 20g **NET CARBS:** 1g **PROTEIN:** 19g

SERVES: 5
SERVING SIZE: ⅓LB (150G)

PREP: 6 MINUTES
PRESSURE: 35 MINUTES
TOTAL: 1 HOUR 10 MINUTES

SETTING: PRESSURE COOK
RELEASE: NATURAL

1½ cups beef broth

2lbs (900g) country-style boneless pork ribs

FOR THE SAUCE

1½ tbsp unsalted butter

1 cup no-sugar-added tomato sauce

1 tbsp apple cider vinegar

1½ tsp liquid smoke

½ tbsp Worcestershire sauce

½ tsp blackstrap molasses

2 tbsp erythritol granular sweetener

1 tsp garlic powder

½ tsp fine grind sea salt

½ tsp onion powder

FOR THE DRY RUB

1 tsp fine grind sea salt

1 tsp ground black pepper

1½ tsp smoked paprika

1½ tsp onion powder

1 tsp garlic powder

1 tsp ground cumin

⅛ tsp cayenne pepper

SAUCY COUNTRY-STYLE BBQ PORK RIBS

These tender boneless ribs are coated in a warm spiced dry rub and then covered in a sweet and smoky low-carb barbecue sauce. They taste slow cooked, but they're made fast in the Instant Pot!

1 Make the sauce by adding the butter to a small saucepan placed over medium heat. Once the butter is melted, add the tomato sauce, vinegar, liquid smoke, Worcestershire sauce, molasses, sweetener, garlic powder, sea salt, and onion powder. Stir until the ingredients are well combined and then remove from the heat. Set aside.

2 Make the dry rub by combining the sea salt, black pepper, paprika, onion powder, garlic powder, cumin, and cayenne pepper in a small bowl. Mix well to combine. Set aside.

3 Add the beef broth to the inner pot and place the steam rack in the pot.

4 Generously sprinkle the dry rub over the pork and gently rub the spices into the meat. Stack the seasoned ribs on the steam rack.

5 Pour half the barbecue sauce over the ribs, reserving the remaining sauce for serving.

6 Cover, lock the lid, and flip the steam release handle to the sealing position. Select **Pressure Cook (High)** and set the cook time for **35 minutes.**

7 When the cook time is complete, allow the pressure to release naturally (about 20 minutes).

8 Open the lid and use tongs to carefully transfer the ribs to a serving plate. Using a pastry brush, brush the reserved sauce over the ribs. Serve warm.

tip *To make this recipe dairy-free, substitute 1 tbsp avocado oil for the butter in the sauce.*

Nutrition per serving
CALORIES: 398 **FAT:** 23g **NET CARBS:** 7g **PROTEIN:** 36g

SERVES: 3
SERVING SIZE: ⅓LB (151G)

PREP: 4 MINUTES
PRESSURE: 6 MINUTES
TOTAL: 10 MINUTES

SETTING: PRESSURE COOK
RELEASE: QUICK

½ medium beefsteak tomato,
cut into 3 slices

½ medium lemon, cut into 3 slices

1lb (450g) fresh wild-caught
Alaskan cod, cut into 3 equal-sized
fillets

½ tsp fine grind sea salt

¼ tsp ground black pepper

1½ tbsp unsalted butter, divided

2 tbsp lemon juice

½ tbsp olive oil

¼ tsp paprika

1 tsp lemon zest

ALASKAN COD
with Lemon Butter

This light and flaky Alaskan cod dinner is seasoned with butter and spices, touched with citrus accents, and served over a bed of tomato and lemon slices. It's very low in carbs and gluten-free.

1 Arrange the tomato and lemon slices in a single layer in the bottom of a 6-inch (15.25cm) round baking dish.

2 Season both sides of the cod fillets with the sea salt and black pepper. Place the fillets on top of tomato and lemon slices.

3 Top each fillet with ½ tbsp butter and then drizzle the lemon juice and olive oil over top of the fillets. Season the fillets with the paprika and then sprinkle the lemon zest over top.

4 Place the steam rack in the inner pot and add 1 cup water to the bottom of the pot. Place the baking dish on top of the rack.

5 Cover, lock the lid, and flip the steam release handle to the sealing position. Select **Pressure Cook (High)** and set the cook time for **6 minutes.**

6 When the cook time is complete, quick release the pressure, open the lid, and carefully grasp the steam rack handles to lift the rack and dish out of the pot.

7 Check the fish for doneness by making a small incision in the flesh. If the flesh is flaky and opaque, the fish is done. If the fish is not done, place it back in the pot and pressure cook for 2 additional minutes.

8 Using a spatula, carefully transfer the fish to a serving platter. Serve warm.

tip *If using frozen cod fillets, increase the cook time to 10 minutes.*

Nutrition per serving
CALORIES: 185 **FAT:** 7g **NET CARBS:** 1g **PROTEIN:** 27g

SLOW COOKED CHILE LIME GARLIC CHICKEN

This easy-to-prepare keto slow cooker recipe is very low in carbs and gluten-free. It features tender, slow cooked chicken with bold and smoky chipotle spices, and sweet citrus accents.

SERVES: 4
SERVING SIZE: 1 THIGH WITH 2 TBSP SAUCE

PREP: 5 MINUTES
COOK: 4 HOURS
TOTAL: 4 HOURS 15 MINUTES

SETTINGS: SLOW COOK/SAUTÉ
RELEASE: NONE

1 Combine the tomato sauce, chicken broth, olive oil, garlic cloves, green chiles, vinegar, lime juice, cilantro, sweetener, chipotle powder, cumin, sea salt, and black pepper in a blender. Pulse until ingredients are well combined.

2 Lightly spray the bottom of the inner pot with nonstick coconut oil spray.

3 Add the chicken thighs to the pot and then pour the sauce over the chicken.

4 Cover and lock the lid, but leave the steam release handle in the venting position. Select **Slow Cook (More)** and set the cook time for **4 hours.**

5 When the cook time is complete, open the lid and transfer the chicken to a serving platter. Select **Sauté (Normal)** and let the sauce simmer in the pot until thickened, about 6-8 minutes.

6 Spoon the sauce over the chicken. Serve hot.

⅓ cup no-sugar-added tomato sauce

¼ cup chicken broth

1½ tbsp olive oil

3 garlic cloves

2½ tbsp canned mild green chiles

1 tbsp apple cider vinegar

4 tbsp lime juice

¼ cup fresh cilantro leaves

1½ tsp erythritol granular sweetener

1 tsp ground chipotle powder

½ tsp ground cumin

1½ tsp fine grind sea salt

¼ tsp ground black pepper

1½lbs (680g) boneless, skinless chicken thighs

tip *If using bone-in frozen chicken thighs, add 1 additional hour to the cook time.*

Nutrition per serving
CALORIES: 260   **FAT:** 12g   **NET CARBS:** 4g   **PROTEIN:** 32g

CREAMY BROCCOLI CHEESE SOUP
with Bacon

This velvety smooth soup is creamy and rich, and features healthy broccoli and smoky crumbled bacon. It's keto-friendly, low in carbs, and extremely addictive!

SERVES: 6
SERVING SIZE: ¾ CUP WITH ½ TBSP BACON

PREP: 6 MINUTES
PRESSURE: 5 MINUTES
TOTAL: 26 MINUTES

SETTINGS: SAUTÉ/PRESSURE COOK/ SAUTÉ/KEEP WARM
RELEASE: NATURAL/QUICK

1 Select **Sauté (Normal).** Once the pot is hot, add the butter and heat until the butter is melted.

2 Add the onions, celery, and garlic. Continue sautéing, stirring continuously, for 5 minutes or until the vegetables have softened.

3 Add the chicken stock and broccoli florets to the pot. Sauté, stirring continuously, until the liquid begins to boil, and then press **Cancel** to turn off the pot.

4 Cover, lock the lid, and flip the steam release handle to the sealing position. Select **Pressure Cook (High)** and set the cook time for **5 minutes.**

5 When the cook time is complete, allow the pressure to release naturally for 10 minutes and then quick release the remaining pressure.

6 Open the lid and add the cream cheese, nutmeg, sea salt, and black pepper. Stir to combine.

7 Select **Sauté (Normal).** Let the soup come to a boil and then slowly add the cheddar and Jack cheeses while continuously stirring. Once the cheese has melted, select **Keep Warm** and stir in the heavy cream.

8 Add the xanthan gum powder (if using) and stir until the soup thickens.

9 Ladle the soup into serving bowls and top each serving with ½ tablespoon crumbled bacon and ½ teaspoon chives. Serve hot.

3 tbsp butter

½ yellow onion, diced

2 stalks celery, diced

3 garlic cloves, minced

3½ cups chicken stock

4 cups chopped fresh broccoli florets

3oz (85g) block-style cream cheese, softened and cubed

½ tsp ground nutmeg

½ tsp fine grind sea salt

1 tsp ground black pepper

3 cups shredded cheddar cheese

½ cup shredded Monterey Jack cheese

2 cups heavy cream

½ tsp xanthan gum (optional)

4 slices cooked bacon, crumbled

1 tbsp finely chopped chives

tip *Xanthan gum is added as a thickening agent and can be omitted from this recipe.*

You can use frozen broccoli florets in place of fresh florets.

Nutrition per serving
CALORIES: 400   **FAT:** 31g   **NET CARBS:** 4g   **PROTEIN:** 18g

SERVES: 4
SERVING SIZE: 2 THIGHS WITH 3 TBSP SAUCE

PREP: 5 MINUTES
PRESSURE: 8 MINUTES
TOTAL: 36 MINUTES

SETTINGS: SAUTÉ/ PRESSURE COOK/SAUTÉ
RELEASE: NATURAL/QUICK

1½lbs (680g) boneless, skinless chicken thighs

½ tsp fine grind sea salt

⅛ tsp ground black pepper

1 tbsp avocado oil

⅔ cup chicken broth

2 tbsp unsalted butter, divided

½ tsp arrowroot powder

3 garlic cloves, minced

1 cup sliced fresh mushrooms

1 tsp tamari sauce

⅓ cup Marsala wine

---

tip *Arrowroot powder is added to thicken the sauce. It can be omitted from the recipe, but the sauce will be thinner.*

CHICKEN MUSHROOM MARSALA

Juicy seared chicken thighs are smothered in a rich and flavorful Marsala wine mushroom sauce in this low-carb, gluten-free, keto version of the classic Italian dish.

1 Season the chicken thighs with the sea salt and black pepper.

2 Select **Sauté (Normal)** and add the avocado oil to the inner pot. Once the oil is hot, add the chicken thighs and sear for 4 minutes per side or until browned. Pour the chicken broth over the chicken thighs.

3 Cover, lock the lid, and flip the steam release handle to the sealing position. Select **Pressure Cook (High)** and set the cook time for **8 minutes.**

4 When the cook time is complete, allow the pressure to release naturally for 5 minutes and then quick release the remaining pressure. Open the lid and transfer the chicken to a plate. Set aside.

5 Carefully remove the inner pot from the base. Drain, rinse, and wipe dry with a paper towel, and then return the pot to the base.

6 Add 1 tbsp butter and the arrowroot powder to a small bowl. Using a fork, mash the arrowroot powder into the butter until the ingredients are thoroughly combined. Set aside.

7 Select **Sauté (More)** and add the remaining butter to pot. Once the butter is melted, add the garlic, mushrooms, and tamari sauce. Sauté for 3 minutes or until the mushrooms soften and begin to brown.

8 Add the wine to the pot and continue sautéing for 3 additional minutes, stirring continuously. Once the sauce is bubbling, add the arrowroot-butter mixture and stir. Continue cooking, stirring continuously, for 1–2 minutes or until the sauce begins to thicken.

9 Add the chicken thighs back to the pot and spoon the sauce over the chicken. Allow the chicken to cook for 3 additional minutes and then press **Cancel** to turn off the pot.

10 Use a large spoon to transfer the chicken and sauce to serving plates. Serve hot.

Nutrition per serving
CALORIES: 400   **FAT:** 17g   **NET CARBS:** 3g   **PROTEIN:** 45g

HERB-RUBBED PORK LOIN ROAST *with Asparagus*

This tender, savory pork roast features an herb rub and marinade, and is low-carb, gluten-free, and dairy-free. It's served with fresh steamed asparagus, which cooks perfectly al dente in the Instant Pot.

1 In a small bowl, combine the smoked paprika, thyme, garlic powder, onion powder, oregano, black pepper, and sea salt. Mix until well combined and then add 1½ tbsp olive oil. Stir until blended.

2 Using a pastry brush, brush all sides of the pork roast with the oil and spice mixture. Place the roast in a covered dish and transfer to the refrigerator to marinate for 20–30 minutes. When the marinating time for the roast is complete, select **Saute (Normal)** and brush the inner pot with remaining olive oil. Once the oil is hot, add the pork roast and sear for 4–5 minutes per side or until browned. Remove the roast from the pot and set aside.

3 Add the onions and garlic to the pot and saute for 2 minutes, or until the onions soften and garlic becomes fragrant. Add the chicken broth and Worcestershire sauce. Using a wooden spoon, stir and scrape the bottom of the pot to loosen any bits. Return the pork roast to the pot.

4 Cover, lock the lid, and flip the steam release handle to the sealing position. Select **Pressure Cook (High)** and set the cook time for **15 minutes.** When the cook time is complete, allow the pressure release naturally for 10 minutes and then quick release the remaining pressure.

5 Open the lid. Check the internal temperature of the roast, which should be between 145°F (63°C) and 160°F (71°C). (If the roast is underdone, replace the lid and pressure cook for 5 additional minutes.) Transfer the roast to a cutting board, cover with aluminum foil, and set aside to rest. Transfer the broth to a measuring cup. Set aside.

6 Place the steam rack in the inner pot and add 1 cup water to the bottom of the pot. Place the asparagus in an ovenproof bowl that will fit in the inner pot and place the bowl on top of the steam rack.

7 Cover, lock the lid, and flip the steam release handle to the sealing position. Select **Steam** and set the cook time for **2 minutes.** Once the cook time is complete, quick release the pressure.

8 Open the lid and use tongs to transfer the asparagus to a large serving platter. Season with additional salt and pepper to taste. Thinly slice the roast and transfer to the serving platter with the asparagus. Drizzle the reserved broth over top. Serve warm.

SERVES: 6
SERVING SIZE: ⅓LB (150G) PORK ROAST WITH 6 ASPARAGUS SPEAR HALVES

PREP: 25 MINUTES
PRESSURE: 17 MINUTES
TOTAL: 50 MINUTES

SETTINGS: SAUTÉ/ PRESSURE COOK/STEAM
RELEASE: NATURAL/QUICK

1½ tsp smoked paprika

1 tsp dried thyme

½ tsp garlic powder

½ tsp onion powder

½ tsp dried oregano

½ tsp ground black pepper

1 tsp fine grind sea salt

2 tbsp olive oil, divided

2lbs (1kg) boneless pork loin roast

½ medium white onion, chopped

2 garlic cloves, minced

⅔ cup chicken broth

2 tbsp Worcestershire sauce

20 fresh asparagus spears, cut in half and woody ends removed

tip *For a bolder flavor, allow the roast to marinate for up to 2 hours.*

Nutrition per serving
CALORIES: 371 **FAT:** 18g **NET CARBS:** 3g **PROTEIN:** 44g

SERVES: 6
SERVING SIZE: ½ CUP PORK WITH ⅓ CUP CABBAGE

PREP: 10 MINUTES
PRESSURE: 1 HOUR 2 MINUTES
TOTAL: 1 HOUR 32 MINUTES

SETTINGS: SAUTÉ/PRESSURE COOK/PRESSURE COOK
RELEASE: NATURAL/QUICK

1½ tbsp olive oil

3lbs (1.4kg) pork shoulder roast, cut into 4 equal-sized pieces

3 cloves garlic, minced

1 tbsp liquid smoke

2 cups water, divided

1 tbsp Hawaiian black lava sea salt or Hawaiian red sea salt

2 cups shredded cabbage

HAWAIIAN PULLED PORK
with Cabbage

This smoky, tender pork has all the rich and vibrant flavors of a Hawaiian luau! Served with a side of cabbage, this recipe is very low in carbs and also paleo-friendly.

1 Select **Sauté (Normal)** and add the olive oil to the inner pot. Once the oil is hot, add the pork cuts and sear for 3–5 minutes per side or until browned. Once browned, transfer the pork to a platter and set aside. Press **Cancel** to turn off the pot.

2 Add the garlic, liquid smoke, and 1½ cups water to the inner pot. Stir to combine.

3 Return the pork to the pot and sprinkle the salt over top.

4 Cover, lock the lid, and flip the steam release handle to the sealing position. Select **Pressure Cook (High)** and set the cook time for **1 hour.** (Note that you may need to increase the cook time for a larger roast.)

5 When the cook time is complete, allow the pressure to release naturally (about 20 minutes).

6 Open the lid and transfer the pork to a large platter. Using two forks, shred the pork. Set aside.

7 Add the shredded cabbage and remaining water to the liquid in the pot. Stir.

8 Cover, lock the lid, and flip the steam release handle to the sealing position. Select **Pressure Cook (High)** and set the cook time for **2 minutes.** When the cook time is complete, quick release the pressure.

9 Transfer the cabbage to the serving platter with the pork. Serve warm.

tip *If your grocer does not carry black or red Hawaiian sea salts, you can substitute equal amounts of coarse grind pink Himalayan sea salt or kosher salt.*

Nutrition per serving
CALORIES: 389 **FAT:** 27g **NET CARBS:** 1g **PROTEIN:** 34g

RICH AND HEARTY BEEF STEW

This hearty, full-bodied stew is comforting and very satisfying on a chilly evening. To keep the carb count low, it's made without potatoes, but you'll never miss them in this mouthwatering stew.

SERVES: 6
SERVING SIZE: 1 CUP

PREP: 5 MINUTES
PRESSURE: 35 MINUTES
TOTAL: 1 HOUR

SETTINGS: SAUTÉ/MEAT STEW
RELEASE: NATURAL/QUICK

1 In a large bowl, combine the chuck roast and arrowroot powder. Use a large spoon to turn and coat the meat in the powder. Set aside.

2 Select **Sauté (Normal)** and add the olive oil to the pot. Once the oil is hot, add the meat and sauté, stirring constantly, for about 5 minutes or until the meat is browned on all sides.

3 Once the meat is browned, add the zucchini, mushrooms, celery, carrots, garlic, tomato sauce, beef broth, thyme, paprika, sea salt, black pepper, rosemary, parsley, garlic powder, celery seed, and onion powder to the pot. Stir well to combine.

4 Cover, lock the lid, and flip the steam release handle to the sealing position. Select **Meat Stew (High)** and set the cook time for **35 minutes.**

5 When the cook time is complete, allow the pressure to release naturally for 15 minutes and then quick release the remaining pressure.

6 Open the lid, stir, and then ladle the stew into serving bowls. Serve hot.

1lb (450g) beef chuck roast, cut into 1-inch (2.5cm) cubes

2 tsp arrowroot powder

1½ tbsp olive oil

1 cup chopped zucchini

1 cup chopped mushrooms

3 ribs celery, sliced

½ cup sliced carrots

2 garlic cloves, minced

¾ cup no-sugar-added tomato sauce

4 cups beef broth

1 tbsp dried thyme

1 tbsp paprika

2½ tsp fine grind sea salt

1 tsp ground black pepper

1 tsp dried rosemary

1 tsp dried parsley

1 tsp garlic powder

1 tsp celery seed

1 tsp onion powder

tip *For an added nutritional boost, replace the beef broth in this recipe with Homemade Bone Broth (see page 81).*

Nutrition per serving
CALORIES: 300 **FAT:** 20g **NET CARBS:** 8g **PROTEIN:** 17g

SERVES: 6
SERVING SIZE: 1 CUP
WITH 4 MEATBALLS

PREP: 10 MINUTES
PRESSURE: 15 MINUTES
TOTAL: 50 MINUTES

SETTINGS: SAUTÉ/PRESSURE COOK
RELEASE: NATURAL/QUICK

1lb (450g) ground beef

1½ tbsp golden flaxseed meal

1 large egg

¼ cup no-sugar-added tomato sauce

⅓ cup shredded mozzarella cheese

1½ tbsp Italian seasoning blend, divided

1½ tsp garlic powder, divided

1½ tsp fine grind sea salt, divided

1 tbsp olive oil

½ medium yellow onion, minced

2 garlic cloves, minced

¼ cup pancetta, diced

1 cup sliced zucchini

1 cup sliced yellow squash

½ cup sliced carrots

14oz (400g) can diced tomatoes

4 cups beef broth

½ tsp ground black pepper

3 tbsp shredded Parmesan cheese

tip *Prebaking the meatballs in the oven helps ensure they won't fall apart while cooking in the pot.*

MEATBALL MINESTRONE SOUP

This warm and comforting soup features vegetables and homemade meatballs in a savory minestrone broth. Pancetta adds a smoky punch to this keto version of a classic Italian soup.

1 Preheat the oven to 400°F (204°C) and line a large baking sheet with aluminum foil.

2 In a large bowl, combine the ground beef, flaxseed meal, egg, tomato sauce, mozzarella, ½ tbsp Italian seasoning, ½ tsp garlic powder, and ½ tsp sea salt. Using your hands, mix the ingredients until well combined.

3 Make the meatballs by shaping 1 heaping tablespoon of the ground beef mixture into a meatball. Repeat with the remaining mixture and then transfer the meatballs to the prepared baking sheet.

4 Place the meatballs in the oven and bake for 15 minutes. When the baking time is complete, remove from the oven and set aside.

5 Select **Sauté (Normal).** Once the pot is hot, add the olive oil, onion, garlic, and pancetta. Sauté, stirring constantly, for 2 minutes or until the garlic becomes fragrant and the onions begin to soften.

6 Add the zucchini, yellow squash, and carrots to the pot. Sauté for 3 additional minutes.

7 Add the diced tomatoes, beef broth, black pepper, and remaining garlic powder, sea salt, and Italian seasoning to the pot. Stir to combine and then add the meatballs.

8 Cover, lock the lid, and flip the steam release handle to the sealing position. Select **Pressure Cook (High)** and set the cook time for **15 minutes.**

9 When the cook time is complete, allow the pressure to release naturally for 10 minutes and then quick release the remaining pressure.

10 Open the lid and gently stir the soup. Ladle into serving bowls and top each serving with ½ tablespoon of the Parmesan. Serve hot.

DINNERS, SOUPS, AND STEWS

Nutrition per serving
CALORIES: 300   **FAT:** 18g   **NET CARBS:** 7g   **PROTEIN:** 23g

SERVES: 5
SERVING SIZE: 1 CUP

PREP: 5 MINUTES
PRESSURE: 13 MINUTES
TOTAL: 50 MINUTES

SETTING: PRESSURE COOK
RELEASE: QUICK

2 cups cauliflower florets

1lb (450g) boneless, skinless chicken thighs

4½ cups chicken broth

1 tbsp unflavored gelatin powder

½ yellow onion, chopped

2 garlic cloves, minced

2 tsp fine grind sea salt

½ tsp ground black pepper

½ cup sliced zucchini

3 celery stalks, chopped

⅓ cup sliced carrots

1 tsp dried parsley

1 tsp dried thyme

1 tsp ground turmeric

½ tsp dried marjoram

½ tsp dried oregano

CHICKEN AND CAULIFLOWER RICE SOUP

Warm and comforting, this keto version of chicken and rice soup is much lower in carbs than the traditional version. Substituting cauliflower rice for white rice makes this a healthy low-carb option.

1 Add the cauliflower florets to a food processor and pulse until a ricelike consistency is achieved. Set aside.

2 Add the chicken thighs, chicken broth, gelatin powder, onions, garlic, sea salt, and black pepper to the pot. Gently stir to combine.

3 Cover, lock the lid, and flip the steam release handle to the sealing position. Select **Pressure Cook (High)** and set the cook time for **10 minutes.**

4 When the cook time is complete, quick release the pressure and open the lid.

5 Transfer only the chicken thighs to a cutting board. Chop the chicken into bite-sized pieces and then return the chopped chicken to the pot.

6 Add the cauliflower rice, zucchini, celery, carrots, parsley, thyme, turmeric, marjoram, and oregano to the pot. Stir to combine.

7 Cover, lock the lid, and flip the steam release handle to the sealing position. Select **Pressure Cook (High)** and set the cook time for **3 minutes.** When the cook time is complete, quick release the pressure.

8 Open the lid. Ladle the soup into serving bowls. Serve hot.

tip *If using frozen chicken thighs, increase the cook time in step 3 to 20 minutes.*

Nutrition per serving
CALORIES: 180   **FAT:** 14g   **NET CARBS:** 4g   **PROTEIN:** 25g

FILIPINO-STYLE CHICKEN ADOBO

This dish features tender, juicy chicken in a flavor-rich, tangy broth with complex and distinct spices. It's a classic Filipino-inspired meal that's simple to make and comes together easily in the Instant Pot.

1 In a medium bowl, combine the chicken broth, tamari sauce, and vinegar. Stir to combine. Set aside.

2 Select **Sauté (Normal)** and add the olive oil to the pot.

3 Once the oil is hot, add the chicken thighs and sauté for 2 minutes per side or until browned.

4 Add the garlic, pour the chicken broth mixture over top, and add the peppercorns and bay leaves.

5 Cover, lock the lid, and flip the steam release handle to the sealing position. Select **Pressure Cook (High)** and set the cook time for **7 minutes.**

6 When the cook time is complete, allow the pressure to release naturally for 10 minutes and then quick release the remaining pressure.

7 Open the lid and stir. Remove and discard the bay leaves and then use a fork to break the chicken into bite-sized pieces. Transfer to a serving plate. Serve hot.

SERVES: 4
SERVING SIZE: ⅔ CUP CHICKEN WITH ⅓ CUP SAUCE

PREP: 4 MINUTES
PRESSURE: 7 MINUTES
TOTAL: 21 MINUTES

SETTINGS: SAUTÉ/PRESSURE COOK
RELEASE: NATURAL/QUICK

⅔ cup chicken broth

⅓ cup tamari sauce

⅓ cup white vinegar

1 tbsp olive oil

2lbs (900g) boneless, skinless chicken thighs

3 garlic cloves, crushed

1 tsp black peppercorns

2 bay leaves

tip *To make this recipe soy-free, substitute an equal amount coconut aminos for the tamari sauce.*

Nutrition per serving
CALORIES: 360 **FAT:** 20g **NET CARBS:** 2g **PROTEIN:** 40g

HEARTY BACON CHEESEBURGER SOUP

Rich, hearty, and satisfying, this soup tastes like a bacon cheeseburger but without all the carbs from a bun! Bacon adds a smoky, robust flavor to this gluten-free, low-carb soup.

 SERVES: 8
SERVING SIZE: 1 CUP

 PREP: 5 MINUTES
PRESSURE: 15 MINUTES
TOTAL: 24 MINUTES

 SETTINGS: SAUTÉ/PRESSURE COOK
RELEASE: QUICK

1 In a blender or food processor, combine the almond milk, onion, garlic, diced tomatoes, tomato paste, oregano, basil, paprika, sea salt, and black pepper. Blend until a smooth consistency is achieved. Set aside.

2 Select **Sauté (Normal)** and add the olive oil to the pot. Once the oil is hot, crumble the ground beef into the pot. Sauté, stirring continuously, for 2 minutes or until the beef is browned.

3 Place a large colander over a heat-safe bowl. Carefully remove the inner pot from the base and transfer the browned beef to the colander to drain off any excess fat. Return the drained beef to the pot and add the bacon. Stir.

4 Add the tomato mixture and beef broth to the pot. Stir. Add the zucchini, yellow squash, and mushrooms. Stir again and then press **Cancel** to turn off the pot.

5 Cover, lock the lid, and flip the steam release handle to the sealing position. Select **Pressure Cook (High)** and set the cook time for **15 minutes.** When the cook time is complete, quick release the pressure.

6 Open the lid. Add the heavy cream and stir until well incorporated. Replace the lid and allow the soup to warm in the pot for 4–5 minutes.

7 Open the lid and ladle the soup into serving bowls. Top each serving with 1 tablespoon of the cheddar cheese. Serve warm.

¾ cup unsweetened almond milk

½ medium yellow onion, peeled and chopped

2 garlic cloves, minced

28oz (800g) can diced tomatoes

6oz (170g) can no-sugar-added tomato paste

½ tsp dried oregano

½ tsp dried basil

½ tsp paprika

1 tsp fine grind sea salt

½ tsp freshly ground black pepper

1 tbsp olive oil

1lb (450g) ground beef

5 slices cooked bacon, chopped

3 cups beef broth

1 cup sliced zucchini

1 cup sliced yellow squash

1 cup sliced mushrooms

⅓ cup heavy cream

½ cup shredded cheddar cheese

tip *To make this recipe dairy-free, substitute ⅓ cup coconut cream for the heavy cream and ½ cup shredded almond cheese for the cheddar.*

Nutrition per serving
CALORIES: 285 **FAT:** 17g **NET CARBS:** 9g **PROTEIN:** 19g

SERVES: 6
SERVING SIZE: 1 CUP

PREP: 5 MINUTES
PRESSURE: 5 MINUTES
TOTAL: 18 MINUTES

SETTINGS: SAUTÉ/
PRESSURE COOK/SAUTÉ
RELEASE: NATURAL/QUICK

2 tbsp unsalted butter, divided

½lb (225g) medium uncooked shrimp, peeled and deveined

½ medium yellow onion, diced

2 cloves garlic, minced

4 cups chicken broth

2 tbsp lime juice

2 tbsp fish sauce

2½ tsp red curry paste

2 tbsp tamari sauce

1 stalk lemongrass, outer stalk removed, bruised (crushed), and finely chopped

1 cup sliced fresh white mushrooms

1 tbsp freshly grated ginger root

1 tsp fine grind sea salt

½ tsp ground black pepper

13.5oz (400ml) can unsweetened, full-fat coconut milk

3 tbsp chopped fresh cilantro

THAI-STYLE SHRIMP SOUP

This creamy soup features shrimp in a rich broth with accents of coconut, lime, and fragrant lemongrass. It's low in carbs and features a lovely blend of Thai flavors and spices.

1 Select **Sauté (Normal)**. Once the pot becomes hot, add 1 tbsp butter.

2 Once the butter is melted, add the shrimp and sauté, stirring continuously, for 3 minutes or until the shrimp turns opaque. Immediately transfer the shrimp to a medium bowl. Set aside.

3 Add the remaining butter to the pot. Once the butter is melted, add the onions and garlic and sauté for 2 minutes or until the garlic is fragrant and the onions begin to soften. Press **Cancel** to turn off the pot.

4 Add the chicken broth, lime juice, fish sauce, red curry paste, tamari sauce, lemongrass, mushrooms, ginger root, sea salt, and black pepper to the pot. Stir to combine.

5 Cover, lock the lid, and flip the steam release handle to the sealing position. Select **Pressure Cook (High)** and set the cook time for **5 minutes.**

6 When the cook time is complete, allow the pressure to release naturally for 5 minutes and then quick release the remaining pressure.

7 Open the lid. Add the cooked shrimp and coconut milk. Stir.

8 Select **Sauté (High).** Bring the soup to a boil and then press **Cancel** to turn off the pot. Let the soup rest in the pot for 2 minutes.

9 Ladle the soup into bowls and sprinkle the cilantro over top. Serve hot.

tip *To make this recipe soy-free, substitute 2 tbsp coconut aminos for the tamari sauce.*

To make this recipe dairy-free, substitute 2 tbsp avocado oil for the butter.

Nutrition per serving
CALORIES: 200   **FAT:** 11g   **NET CARBS:** 4g   **PROTEIN:** 13g

SPICY CHICKEN QUESO SOUP

Slightly spicy, cheesy, and full of flavor, this comforting chicken soup is low in carbs, gluten-free, and full of warm spices. The healthy fats in this satisfying soup will help keep you feeling full for longer.

SERVES: 6
SERVING SIZE: 1 CUP

PREP: 5 MINUTES
PRESSURE: 20 MINUTES
TOTAL: 40 MINUTES

SETTINGS: PRESSURE COOK/SAUTÉ
RELEASE: NATURAL/QUICK

1 Combine the chicken broth, salsa, sea salt, garlic powder, chipotle powder, black pepper, coriander, cumin, and parsley in the inner pot. Stir until well combined. Add the chicken thighs to the pot.

2 Cover, lock the lid, and flip the steam release handle to the sealing position. Select **Pressure Cook (High)** and set the cook time for **20 minutes.**

3 When the cook time is complete, allow the pressure to release naturally for 10 minutes and then quick release the remaining pressure.

4 Open the lid, use a slotted spoon to transfer the chicken thighs to a cutting board, and use two forks to shred the chicken. Return the shredded chicken to the pot. Stir to combine.

5 Select **Sauté (High).** Bring the soup to a boil and then add the cream cheese. Whisk continuously until the cream cheese is melted. (Note that small bits of unmelted cream cheese may remain, which is fine.)

6 Press **Cancel** to turn off the pot. Add the Jack cheese and stir until the cheese is melted into the soup.

7 Ladle the soup into bowls. Sprinkle ½ tbsp queso fresco over each serving and top with 1 tsp chopped cilantro (if using). Serve hot.

3 cups chicken broth

1⅓ cups chunky salsa

1 tsp fine grind sea salt

1 tsp garlic powder

½ tsp ground chipotle powder

½ tsp ground black pepper

½ tsp ground coriander

½ tsp ground cumin

½ dried parsley

1lb (450g) boneless skinless chicken thighs

8oz (225g) block-style cream cheese, softened and cubed

½ cup Monterey Jack cheese

¼ cup queso fresco, crumbled

2 tbsp chopped cilantro, to garnish (optional)

tip *You can use mild, medium, or hot salsa varieties to adjust the spiciness to your taste preferences.*

Nutrition per serving
CALORIES: 317 **FAT:** 21g **NET CARBS:** 6g **PROTEIN:** 23g

SERVES: 5
SERVING SIZE: 1 CUP

PREP: 10 MINUTES
PRESSURE: 20 MINUTES
TOTAL: 50 MINUTES

SETTINGS: SAUTÉ/PRESSURE COOK
RELEASE: NATURAL/QUICK

2 tbsp olive oil

1lb (450g) boneless, skinless chicken thighs, cut into bite-sized pieces

½ medium yellow onion, diced

4 garlic cloves, minced

2 jalapeño peppers, stems and seeds removed, chopped

½ cup diced fresh tomato

5 cups chicken broth

Juice of 2 limes

2 tsp fine grind sea salt

1 tsp chili powder

½ tsp garlic powder

¼ tsp ground black pepper

1 medium avocado, chopped

⅓ cup shredded pepper Jack cheese

2 tbsp chopped fresh cilantro (optional)

MEXICAN CHILE LIME CHICKEN SOUP

This Yucatan-inspired, low-carb version of Sopa De Lima (soup of the lime) brings the enticing flavors of the Mayan Riviera to your table with bold flavors and spices tamed by accents of lime,

1 Select **Sauté (normal)** and add the olive oil to inner pot. Once the oil is hot, add the chicken and sauté for 3 minutes per side or until browned.

2 Add the onions, garlic, and jalapeños to the pot. Continue sautéing, stirring continuously, until the vegetables begin to soften.

3 Add the diced tomatoes, chicken broth, lime juice, sea salt, chili powder, garlic powder, and black pepper. Stir to combine.

4 Cover, lock the lid, and flip the steam release handle to the sealing position. Select **Pressure Cook (High)** and set the cook time for **20 minutes.**

5 When the cook time is complete, allow the pressure to release naturally for 15 minutes and then quick release the remaining pressure.

6 Open the lid and ladle the soup into serving bowls. Top each serving with equal amounts of the avocado and pepper Jack, and garnish with the chopped cilantro (if using). Serve hot.

tip *To make this recipe dairy-free, substitute ⅓ cup shredded almond cheese for the pepper Jack or simply omit the cheese.*

If you prefer less heat, you can substitute a milder chile pepper for the jalapeños.

Nutrition per serving
CALORIES: 285   **FAT:** 16g   **NET CARBS:** 3g   **PROTEIN:** 25g

SERVES: 8
SERVING SIZE: 1 CUP

PREP: 5 MINUTES
PRESSURE: 8 MINUTES
TOTAL: 26 MINUTES

SETTINGS: SAUTÉ/PRESSURE COOK
RELEASE: NATURAL/QUICK

2 tbsp butter

½ medium yellow onion, finely chopped

2 garlic cloves, minced

2 celery stalks, finely chopped

½ cup finely chopped carrots

4 cups chicken broth

28oz (800g) can diced tomatoes

3 tbsp tomato paste

12oz (340g) jar roasted red bell pepper strips, drained

½ cup heavy cream

1½ tsp erythritol sweetener blend

2 tsp fine grind sea salt

½ tsp ground black pepper

2 tbsp full-fat sour cream (optional)

ROASTED RED PEPPER AND TOMATO SOUP

Warm and comforting, this creamy, colorful, low-carb soup is bursting with flavor and features a smoky, peppery flavor from roasted bell peppers that is balanced by the sweetness of the tomatoes.

1 Select **Sauté (Normal).** Once the pot is hot, add the butter.

2 Once the butter is melted, add the onions, garlic, celery, and carrots to the pot. Sauté for 3 minutes or until the garlic becomes fragrant and the onions begin to soften.

3 Add the chicken broth, diced tomatoes (with canning liquid), tomato paste, and roasted bell peppers to the pot. Stir to combine.

4 Cover, lock the lid, and flip the steam release handle to the sealing position. Select **Pressure Cook (High)** and set the cook time for **8 minutes.**

5 When the cook time is complete, allow the pressure to release naturally for 10 minutes and then quick release the remaining pressure.

6 Open the lid and add the heavy cream and sweetener. Using an immersion blender, purée the soup until a smooth consistency is achieved and no lumps remain.

7 Ladle the soup into serving bowls. Season with the salt and pepper, stir, and then top each serving with 1 teaspoon of the sour cream (if using). Serve hot.

tip *To make this recipe dairy-free, substitute ½ cup unsweetened full-fat coconut milk for the heavy cream and 2 tbsp avocado oil for the butter.*

Nutrition per serving
CALORIES: 220   **FAT:** 14g   **NET CARBS:** 8g   **PROTEIN:** 5g

CHUNKY BEEF AND VEGGIE CHILI

This robust and hearty, bean-free chili has warm, fragrant spices, tender beef, and nutrient-rich vegetables to keep you full. The Instant Pot does a beautiful job of cooking this rich and satisfying chili!

SERVES: 5
SERVING SIZE:
⅔ CUP CHILI WITH TOPPINGS

PREP: 5 MINUTES
PRESSURE: 25 MINUTES
TOTAL: 45 MINUTES

SETTINGS: SAUTÉ/PRESSURE COOK
RELEASE: NATURAL/QUICK

1 Select **Sauté (Normal).** Once the pot is hot, add the olive oil and ground beef and sauté for 6 minutes or until the beef is browned, using a wooden spoon to stir and break up the beef.

2 Add the onions and garlic to the pot. Sauté for 3 minutes, stirring occasionally, until the garlic becomes fragrant and the onions begin to soften.

3 Add the chili powder, cumin, sea salt, paprika, garlic powder, coriander powder, cayenne pepper, water, diced tomatoes (with canning liquid), tomato paste, cauliflower, and zucchini to the pot. Stir to combine.

4 Cover, lock the lid, and flip the steam release handle to the sealing position. Select **Pressure Cook (High)** and set the cook time for **25 minutes.**

5 When the cook time is complete, allow the pressure to release naturally for 10 minutes and then quick release the remaining pressure.

6 Open the lid and stir. Ladle the chili into serving bowls and top each serving with 2 tablespoons cheddar cheese, 2 tablespoons avocado, and ½ tablespoon sour cream. Serve hot.

½ tbsp olive oil

1¼lb (567g) ground beef

½ medium yellow onion, chopped

2 garlic cloves, minced

1½ tbsp chili powder

2 tsp ground cumin

1 tsp fine grind sea salt

1 tsp smoked paprika

1 tsp garlic powder

¼ tsp coriander powder

⅛ tsp cayenne pepper

⅔ cup water

1½ cups canned diced tomatoes

4 tbsp tomato paste

⅔ cup finely chopped cauliflower

1 cup diced zucchini

⅔ cup grated cheddar cheese

½ medium avocado, chopped

2½ tbsp full-fat sour cream

tip *To make this recipe dairy-free, substitute an equal amount of shredded almond cheese for the cheddar, and omit the sour cream.*

Nutrition per serving
CALORIES: 420 **FAT:** 30g **NET CARBS:** 7g **PROTEIN:** 26g

CREAMY PUMPKIN SOUP

Warm, creamy, and savory, this classic pumpkin soup is low carb and simple to make in the Instant Pot. Pumpkin is naturally low in carbs, but you don't have to wait until fall to enjoy this soup.

SERVES: 5
SERVING SIZE: 1 CUP

PREP: 5 MINUTES
COOK: 5 MINUTES
TOTAL: 18 MINUTES

SETTING: SAUTÉ
RELEASE: NONE

1 Select **Sauté (Normal).** Once the pot becomes hot, add the butter and olive oil.

2 Once the butter is melted, add the onions and garlic and sauté for 4 minutes or until the garlic becomes fragrant and the onions begin to soften.

3 Add the pumpkin pureé, chicken broth, sea salt, and black pepper. Stir to combine.

4 Using an immersion blender or hand mixer, blend until a smooth consistency is achieved and no lumps remain. Press **Cancel** to turn off the pot. Stir.

5 Let the soup cool in the pot for 3 minutes and then stir in the heavy cream. (Make sure not to add the cream before the soup has cooled.)

6 Ladle the soup into serving bowls and garnish each serving with ½ tbsp sour cream (if using). Serve warm.

3 tbsp unsalted butter

1 tbsp olive oil

½ medium yellow onion, chopped

2 garlic cloves, roughly chopped

15oz (420g) can no-sugar-added pumpkin purée

3 cups chicken broth

2 tsp fine grind sea salt

½ tsp ground black pepper

⅔ cup heavy cream

3 tbsp full-fat sour cream (optional)

tip *To make this recipe dairy-free, omit the sour cream and substitute 3 tbsp avocado oil for the butter and ⅔ cup full-fat coconut milk for the heavy cream.*

Nutrition per serving
CALORIES: 283   **FAT:** 24g   **NET CARBS:** 7g   **PROTEIN:** 5g

SERVES: 6
SERVING SIZE:
¾ CUP WITH 2 TBSP MOZZARELLA

PREP: 8 MINUTES
PRESSURE: 22 MINUTES
TOTAL: 50 MINUTES

SETTINGS: SAUTÉ/PRESSURE COOK
RELEASE: NATURAL/QUICK

1½ cups cauliflower florets

1 tbsp olive oil

3 garlic cloves, minced

¼ cup diced yellow onion

1lb (450g) ground beef

⅔ cup no-sugar-added tomato sauce

2 tsp fine grind sea salt

1½ tsp garlic powder

1 tsp paprika

1 tsp dried parsley

1 tsp dried oregano

1 tsp ground black pepper

3½ cups beef broth

½ medium head green cabbage, chopped

¾ cup shredded mozzarella cheese

(UN)STUFFED CABBAGE ROLL STEW

Warm and comforting, this flavorful keto stew has wonderful cabbage flavor and is loaded with healthy ingredients. It has all the flavor and taste of cabbage rolls but without all the work!

1 Add the cauliflower florets to a food processor, and pulse until a ricelike texture is achieved. Set aside.

2 Select **Sauté (Normal)** and add the olive oil to the pot. Once the oil is hot, add the onions and garlic and sauté for 4 minutes or until the garlic becomes fragrant and the onions begin to soften.

3 Crumble the ground beef into the pot. Sauté for 5 minutes or until the beef is browned and cooked through completely.

4 Add the tomato sauce, sea salt, garlic powder, paprika, parsley, oregano, and black pepper to the pot. Stir to combine.

5 Add the riced cauliflower, beef broth, and cabbage. Gently stir.

6 Cover, lock the lid, and flip the steam release handle to the sealing position. Select **Pressure Cook (High)** and set the cook time for **22 minutes.**

7 When the cook time is complete, allow the pressure to release naturally for 10 minutes and then quick release the remaining pressure.

8 Ladle the stew into serving bowls and sprinkle 2 tbsp mozzarella over top of each serving. Serve hot.

tip *To make this recipe dairy-free, substitute ¾ cup shredded almond cheese for the mozzarella or simply omit the cheese.*

Nutrition per serving
CALORIES: 250   **FAT:** 14g   **NET CARBS:** 7g   **PROTEIN:** 22g

HOMEMADE BONE BROTH

Warm, nourishing, and full of healthy nutrients, this homemade bone broth is extremely low in carbs and very versatile for making soups and stews, or simply enjoyed on its own as a healthy beverage.

SERVES: 5
SERVING SIZE: 1 CUP

PREP: 5 MINUTES
PRESSURE: 2 HOURS
TOTAL: 2 HOURS 25 MINUTES

SETTING: SOUP/BROTH
RELEASE: NATURAL

1 Place the bones in the pot. Add the celery, carrot, onion, garlic, turmeric, vinegar, sea salt, black peppercorns, thyme, and rosemary.

2 Add the water to the pot. (Make sure the water is at least 1 inch (2.5cm) below the max fill line marked on the inner pot.)

3 Cover, lock the lid, and flip the steam release handle to the sealing position. Select **Soup Broth (High)** and set the cook time for **2 hours.**

4 When the cook time is complete, allow the pressure to release naturally (about 20 minutes).

5 Place a fine mesh sieve over a large bowl. Open the lid, carefully remove the inner pot from the base, and strain the broth through the sieve. Discard the solids and let the broth cool in the bowl for a minimum of 20 minutes.

6 Serve warm or transfer the cooled broth to a large sealable mason jar, tightly seal, and store in the refrigerator for up to 7 days.

1½lbs (680g) assorted meat bones

2 celery stalks, cut into large pieces

1 medium carrot, thickly sliced

½ yellow onion, cut in half

2 garlic cloves

2 small pieces fresh turmeric root

1 tbsp apple cider vinegar

1 tsp fine grind sea salt

½ tsp black peppercorns

2 sprigs fresh thyme

1 sprig fresh rosemary

5½ cups water

tip *A layer of gelatinized fat will form on the surface of the chilled broth. The fat will liquefy once the broth is warmed, but it can be removed with a spoon and discarded, if desired.*

Nutrition per serving
CALORIES: 50   **FAT:** 3g   **NET CARBS:** 0g   **PROTEIN:** 2g

SIDES AND SALADS

SERVES: 2
SERVING SIZE:
2 CUPS SALAD WITH ¼LB (115G)
CHICKEN STRIPS AND
2 TBSP DRESSING

PREP: 6 MINUTES
PRESSURE: 9 MINUTES
TOTAL: 21 MINUTES

SETTINGS: SAUTÉ/PRESSURE COOK
RELEASE: QUICK

½lb (225g) uncooked chicken breast tenders

¼ tsp fine grind sea salt

¼ tsp ground black pepper

1 tbsp avocado oil

½ cup chicken broth

⅓ cup salsa verde

4 cup spring mix lettuce

2 mini bell peppers, tops and seeds removed, chopped

1 Roma tomato, diced

3 tbsp sliced black olives

¼ cup shredded cheddar cheese

1 tbsp chopped cilantro

FOR THE DRESSING

⅓ medium avocado, chopped

2 tbsp full-fat sour cream

2 tbsp salsa verde

1 tbsp lime juice

2 tsp water

1 tbsp chopped cilantro

SALSA VERDE CHICKEN SALAD
with Avocado Lime Dressing

This Mexican-inspired keto salad is light but filling. It features warm chicken strips in a sweet and mild verde sauce served over a fresh green salad and topped with a creamy avocado dressing.

1 Season both sides of the chicken with the sea salt and black pepper.

2 Select **Sauté (Normal).** Once the pot is hot, add the avocado oil and chicken tenders and sauté for 3 minutes per side or until browned. Press **Cancel** to turn off heat.

3 Pour the chicken broth and salsa verde over top of the chicken.

4 Cover, lock the lid, and flip the steam release handle to the sealing position. Select **Pressure Cook (High)** and set the cook time for **9 minutes.**

5 While the chicken is cooking, make the dressing by combining the avocado, sour cream, salsa verde, lime juice, water, and cilantro in a blender. Pulse until a smooth consistency is achieved. Set aside.

6 When the cook time for the chicken is complete, quick release the pressure, open the lid, and transfer the chicken to a platter. Set aside.

7 Place equal amounts of spring mix lettuce on two plates and top the salads with equal amounts of the mini bell peppers.

8 Top each salad with ¼lb (115g) chicken, ½ tbsp of broth from the pot, and equal amounts of the tomatoes, olives, and cheddar.

9 Drizzle 2 tbsp of the dressing over top of each salad and garnish with the chopped cilantro. Serve promptly.

tip *If you don't like the taste of cilantro, you can omit it or replace it in each recipe with ½ tbsp flat-leaf parsley combined with ½ tsp dried Mexican oregano.*

Nutrition per serving
CALORIES: 379 **FAT:** 20g **NET CARBS:** 3g **PROTEIN:** 32g

BACON CHEESEBURGER SALAD
with Thousand Island Dressing

This keto-friendly salad has all the cheeseburger and smoky bacon flavors you love, but without the bun and all the carbs! It's topped with a creamy, low-carb Thousand Island dressing.

SERVES: 2
SERVING SIZE: 2 CUPS SALAD WITH ⅓ CUP TOPPING AND 2 TBSP DRESSING

PREP: 4 MINUTES
COOK: 20 MINUTES
TOTAL: 30 MINUTES

SETTING: SAUTÉ
RELEASE: NONE

1 Make the dressing by combining the mayonnaise, tomato paste, pickle relish, onion powder, parsley, and Worcestershire sauce in a small bowl. Mix well to combine. Cover and refrigerate.

2 Select **Sauté (Normal)**. Once the pot becomes hot, add the bacon slices and sauté for 5–6 minutes per side, or until the bacon becomes crisp. Transfer to a plate lined with a paper towel, let drain, and then chop into bite-sized pieces. Set aside.

3 Crumble the ground beef into the pot and sauté for 6 minutes or until the beef is browned and cooked through completely.

4 Add the garlic powder, sea salt, paprika, and black pepper to the pot. Stir and then promptly press **Cancel** to turn off the heat.

5 Place a colander over a large glass bowl and transfer the mixture to the colander to drain. Set aside.

6 Place equal amounts of the spring mix lettuce on two plates.

7 Top each salad with equal amounts of the ground beef mixture, chopped bacon, tomato, and cheddar cheese.

8 Drizzle 2 tbsp of the dressing over top of each salad. Serve promptly.

2 slices uncooked bacon
⅓ lb (150g) ground beef
¼ tsp garlic powder
¼ tsp fine grind sea salt
¼ tsp paprika
⅛ tsp ground black pepper
4 cups spring mix lettuce
½ medium Roma tomato, diced
3 tbsp shredded cheddar cheese

FOR THE DRESSING
¼ cup mayonnaise
½ tbsp tomato paste
1 tbsp dill pickle relish
½ tsp onion powder
¼ tsp dried parsley
1 tsp Worcestershire sauce

tip *To make this recipe dairy-free, substitute 3 tbsp shredded almond cheese for the cheddar cheese or just omit the cheese.*

Nutrition per serving
CALORIES: 409   **FAT:** 34g   **NET CARBS:** 1g   **PROTEIN:** 23g

FAUX POTATO CAULIFLOWER SALAD

This rich and creamy salad is made without potatoes! This keto take on a classic uses low-carb chopped cauliflower to replace the high-carb potatoes, but it still has all the classic potato salad flavors.

SERVES: 6
SERVING SIZE: ½ CUP

PREP: 6 MINUTES
PRESSURE: 9 MINUTES
TOTAL: 21 MINUTES

SETTINGS: PRESSURE COOK/STEAM
RELEASE: NATURAL/QUICK

1 medium head cauliflower, chopped into bite-sized pieces
4 large eggs
½ cup mayonnaise
1½ tbsp prepared yellow mustard
2½ tbsp dill pickle relish
½ tsp fine grind sea salt
¼ tsp ground black pepper
1 tbsp chopped chives
⅛ tsp paprika

1 Place the steam rack in the inner pot and add 1 cup water to the bottom of the pot. Place the eggs on top of the rack.

2 Cover, lock the lid, and flip the steam release handle to the sealing position. Select **Pressure Cook (High)** and set the cook time for **6 minutes.**

3 While the eggs are cooking, create an ice water bath by filling a large bowl halfway with cold water and ice. Set aside.

4 When the cook time for the eggs is complete, allow the pressure to release naturally for 5 minutes and then quick release the remaining pressure. Press **Cancel** to turn off the pot.

5 Open the lid and use tongs to carefully transfer the eggs to the ice water bath to cool for 5 minutes. Remove the cooled eggs from the bath, peel and chop, and set aside.

6 Remove the inner pot from the base, drain, and then return the pot to the base. Place a steamer basket with legs in the inner pot and add 1 cup cold water to the bottom of the pot.

7 Place the chopped cauliflower in the steamer basket.

8 Cover, lock the lid, and flip the steam release handle to the sealing position. Select **Steam (High)** and set the cook time for **3 minutes.**

9 When the cook time is complete, quick release the pressure, open the lid, and carefully remove the steamer basket from the pot. Transfer the cauliflower to a large bowl.

10 To the bowl with the cauliflower, add the chopped eggs, mayonnaise, mustard, pickle relish, sea salt, and black pepper. Stir to combine.

11 Garnish with the chives and sprinkle the paprika over top. Serve promptly.

tip *If you don't have a steamer basket with legs, you can cook the cauliflower in an ovenproof bowl placed on top of the steam rack.*

Nutrition per serving
CALORIES: 206   **FAT:** 17g   **NET CARBS:** 4g   **PROTEIN:** 7g

SERVES: 2
SERVING SIZE:
2 CUPS WITH ¼LB (115G) SHRIMP

PREP: 6 MINUTES
PRESSURE: 6 MINUTES
TOTAL: 23 MINUTES

SETTINGS: PRESSURE COOK/SAUTÉ
RELEASE: NATURAL/QUICK

½lb (225g) fresh, wild-caught shrimp, peeled and deveined, rinsed and patted dry

1½ tbsp lemon juice

1 garlic clove, minced

⅛ tsp fine grind sea salt

⅛ tsp ground black pepper

1 large egg

¼ cup diced pancetta

4 cups chopped Romaine lettuce

½ medium avocado, chopped

¼ cup shaved Parmesan cheese

FOR THE DRESSING

1½ tbsp full-fat sour cream

1 tbsp mayonnaise

½ tbsp extra virgin olive oil

1 garlic clove, minced

1 tsp fish sauce

1 tbsp lemon juice

½ tbsp grated Parmesan cheese

⅛ tsp fine grind sea salt

⅛ tsp ground black pepper

tip *For a hard-boiled egg, increase the pressure cooking time to 9 minutes.*

GARLIC LEMON SHRIMP CAESAR SALAD

This satisfying salad is low in carbs, gluten-free, and features sautéed shrimp, accents of citrus and garlic, and smoky seared pancetta in a creamy homemade Caesar dressing along with a soft-boiled egg.

1 In a medium bowl, combine the shrimp, lemon juice, garlic, sea salt, and black pepper. Gently toss to coat the shrimp in the seasonings. Set aside.

2 Make the dressing by combining the sour cream, mayonnaise, olive oil, garlic, fish sauce, lemon juice, Parmesan, sea salt, and black pepper in a small bowl. Whisk until blended. Cover and refrigerate.

3 Place the steam rack in the inner pot and add 1 cup water to the bottom of the pot. Place the egg on the rack.

4 Cover, lock the lid, and flip the steam release handle to the sealing position. Select **Pressure Cook (Low)** and set the cook time for **6 minutes.**

5 While the egg is cooking, create an ice water bath by filling a large bowl halfway with cold water and ice. Set aside.

6 When the cook time for the egg is complete, allow the pressure to release naturally for 2 minutes and then quick release the remaining pressure.

7 Open the lid and use tongs to transfer the egg to the ice water bath. Let the egg cool in the bath for 6 minutes.

8 Select **Sauté (Normal)**. Once the pot is hot, add the pancetta and sauté for 4–5 minutes or until the pancetta begins to brown on the edges. Transfer the pancetta to a small bowl. Set aside.

9 Add the shrimp to the pot and cook for 2 minutes per side or until the shrimp become opaque. Transfer to a medium bowl. Set aside.

10 In a large bowl, combine the Romaine, shrimp, pancetta, and avocado. Pour the dressing over the salad and gently toss to combine. Divide equal amounts of the salad between two plates.

11 Sprinkle ⅛ cup of the shaved Parmesan over each salad. Remove the egg from ice bath, peel, slice in half lengthwise, and place half an egg on top of each salad. Serve promptly.

Nutrition per serving
CALORIES: 465 **FAT:** 31g **NET CARBS:** 3g **PROTEIN:** 40g

MEXICAN BEEF TACO SALAD

This keto-friendly salad has everything you'd want in a taco but without all the carbs. It features wonderful taco toppings on a crunchy salad and is topped with a homemade Catalina dressing.

SERVES: 2
SERVING SIZE: 2 CUPS SALAD WITH ½ CUP TACO MEAT AND 2 TBSP DRESSING

PREP: 5 MINUTES
COOK: 8 MINUTES
TOTAL: 15 MINUTES

SETTING: SAUTÉ
RELEASE: NONE

1 Make the dressing by combining the avocado oil, vinegar, Worcestershire sauce, tomato sauce, onion powder, paprika, sweetener, and sea salt in a small bowl. Whisk until blended. Set aside.

2 Select **Sauté (Normal).** Once the pot is hot, add the avocado oil. Crumble the ground beef into the pot and sauté for 5 minutes, stirring frequently, until the meat is browned and cooked through.

3 Add the tomato sauce, water, chili powder, cumin, garlic powder, onion powder, paprika, and sea salt to the pot. Stir.

4 Continue cooking, stirring continuously, until the sauce begins to bubble and then press **Cancel** to turn off the pot. Let the ground beef rest in the pot for 3 minutes to allow the sauce to thicken.

5 Divide equal amounts of lettuce between two plates. Spoon ½ cup of the ground beef mixture over top of the lettuce and top each salad with equal amounts of the tomato, avocado, olives, and cheddar.

6 Drizzle 2 tbsp of the dressing over top of each salad and then top each with 1 tablespoon of the sour cream. Serve promptly.

1 tbsp avocado oil

½ lb (225g) ground beef

¼ cup no-sugar-added tomato sauce

2 tbsp water

1½ tsp chili powder

½ tsp ground cumin

¼ tsp garlic powder

⅛ tsp onion powder

⅛ tsp paprika

¼ tsp fine grind sea salt

½ medium head iceberg lettuce, torn into small pieces (about 4 cups)

1 Roma tomato, diced

½ medium avocado, diced

2 tbsp sliced black olives

¼ cup shredded cheddar cheese

2 tbsp full-fat sour cream

FOR THE DRESSING

1½ tbsp avocado oil

1 tbsp apple cider vinegar

¼ tsp Worcestershire sauce

1½ tbsp no-sugar-added tomato sauce

¼ tsp onion powder

¼ tsp paprika

⅛ tsp erythritol granular sweetener

⅛ tsp fine grind sea salt

tip *If you're missing some seasoning ingredients, you can substitute 1 tablespoon store-bought taco seasoning in step 3 and omit the chili powder, cumin, garlic powder, onion powder, paprika, and sea salt.*

Nutrition per serving
CALORIES: 504 **FAT:** 38g **NET CARBS:** 7g **PROTEIN:** 30g

SERVES: 4
SERVING SIZE:
1 SALAD WITH ¼LB (113G) STEAK

PREP: 6 MINUTES
PRESSURE: 29 MINUTES
TOTAL: 1 HOUR

SETTINGS: SAUTÉ/
PRESSURE COOK/STEAM
RELEASE: NATURAL/QUICK

1lb (450g) skirt steak, cut into 4 equal-sized steaks

1 tsp fine grind sea salt

¼ tsp ground black pepper

1 tbsp avocado oil

¼ cup olive oil

2 tbsp lime juice

1 tbsp tamari sauce

2 garlic cloves, minced

1 tsp ground cumin

½ tsp chili powder

¼ tsp dried oregano

4 mini bell peppers, stems and seeds removed, sliced into thin strips

2 jalapeño peppers, stems and seeds removed, sliced into thin strips

4 cups romaine lettuce, chopped into bite-sized pieces

4 cups spring lettuce mix

1 medium avocado, sliced

4 tbsp chopped fresh cilantro

FOR THE DRESSING

⅓ cup full-fat sour cream

2 tbsp mayonnaise

2 garlic cloves

3 tbsp lime juice

1½ tbsp apple cider vinegar

1 tsp fine grind sea salt

¼ tsp ground black pepper

⅓ cup fresh cilantro

STEAK FAJITA SALAD
with Cilantro Lime Dressing

This hearty salad is low in carbs and has all the flavors of traditional steak fajitas, but without the tortillas. The tender and flavorful steak is accented by a zesty, creamy dressing and touched with hints of lime.

1 Make the dressing by combining the sour cream, mayonnaise, garlic cloves, lime juice, vinegar, sea salt, black pepper, and cilantro in a food processor or blender. Pulse until the ingredients are combined and a smooth, creamy consistency is achieved. Transfer the dressing to a resealable container and place in the refrigerator.

2 Season both sides of the steaks with the sea salt and black pepper. Gently rub the seasonings into the meat.

3 Select **Sauté (Normal).** Once the pot becomes hot, add the avocado oil and heat for 2 minutes. Place the steaks in the inner pot and sauté for 4 minutes per side or until browned. Transfer the steaks to a plate and set aside. Press **Cancel** to turn off the heat.

4 Combine the olive oil, lime juice, tamari sauce, garlic, cumin, chili powder, and oregano in a large 1-gallon (3.785l) zippered freezer bag. Tightly seal and carefully shake the bag to combine the ingredients.

5 Add the steaks to the bag, reseal, and carefully shake the bag to coat the steaks in the marinade. Place the bag with the steaks in the refrigerator to marinate for 20 minutes.

6 Place the steam rack in the inner pot and add 1 cup water to the bottom of the pot. Place a 20-inch (50cm) sheet of aluminum foil over the steam rack and fold the sides of the aluminum foil up. Place the marinated steaks on the rack and drizzle the marinade from the bag over the steaks. Wrap the sides of the foil over the steaks to form a foil packet. (You can stack the steaks if they won't fit in a single layer.)

7 Cover, lock the lid, and flip the steam release handle to the sealing position. Select **Pressure Cook (High)** and set the cook time for **25 minutes.** When the cook time is complete, allow the pressure to release naturally for 5 minutes and then quick release the remaining pressure.

8 Open the lid and transfer the foil packet to a cutting board. Open the top of the foil packet and let the steaks rest for 5 minutes before slicing into thin strips.

Nutrition per serving
CALORIES: 565 **FAT:** 40g **NET CARBS:** 6g **PROTEIN:** 33g

9 While the steaks are resting, remove the steam rack from inner pot. Carefully remove the inner pot from base, drain, and then return the pot to the base. Place a steamer basket with legs in the inner pot and add 1 cup water to the bottom of the pot. Place the bell pepper and jalapeño strips in the steamer basket.

tip *The cook time in this recipe results in a medium doneness for the steak. For medium rare doneness adjust the cook time to 20 minutes. For rare doneness adjust the cook time to 18 minutes.*

10 Cover, lock the lid, and flip the steam release handle to the sealing position. Select **Steam (High)** and set the cook time for **4 minutes**. When the cook time is complete, quick release the pressure, open the lid and transfer the pepper strips to a medium bowl.

11 Add 1 cup romaine and 1 cup spring mix to each of four serving plates. Top each with ¼lb (115g) steak, equal amounts of the pepper strips, and one quarter of the sliced avocado. Drizzle 2 tbsp of the dressing over top and sprinkle 1 tbsp cilantro over each salad. Serve promptly.

SERVES: 4
SERVING SIZE: 2 LETTUCE CUPS

PREP: 5 MINUTES
PRESSURE: 4 MINUTES
TOTAL: 13 MINUTES

SETTINGS: SAUTÉ/PRESSURE COOK
RELEASE: QUICK

½ cup chicken broth

2 tbsp fish sauce

½ tsp erythritol granular sweetener

1 tsp crushed red pepper flakes

½ tsp fine grind sea salt

1½ tbsp avocado oil

2 garlic cloves, minced

1lb (450g) ground pork

16–18 roasted peanuts, shelled

3 tbsp lime juice

3 tbsp chopped mint leaves

3 tbsp chopped cilantro

2 tsp sriracha sauce

8 medium hearts-of-romaine lettuce leaves

2 stalks green onions, chopped (green tips only)

THAI STYLE LARB
in Lettuce Cups

Lively and refreshing, with warm spices that are balanced with a citrus accent, this keto friendly version of a classic Thai dish has a light, nutty crunch and beautiful flavors all served up in a crisp lettuce cup.

1 In a medium bowl, combine the chicken broth, fish sauce, sweetener, red pepper flakes, and sea salt. Mix well. Set aside.

2 Select **Sauté (Normal).** Once the pot is hot, add the avocado oil and garlic. Sauté, stirring continuously, until the garlic becomes fragrant.

3 Crumble the ground pork into the pot and sauté for 4 minutes or until the pork is fully cooked. Pour the chicken broth mixture over the ground pork.

4 Cover, lock the lid, and flip the steam release handle to the sealing position. Select **Pressure Cook (High)** and set the cook time for **4 minutes.**

5 While the pork is cooking, add the roasted peanuts to a food processor and pulse until coarsely ground. Set aside.

6 When the cook time for the pork is complete, quick release the pressure.

7 Open the lid and add the lime juice, mint, cilantro, and sriracha sauce. Stir to combine.

8 Arrange the lettuce leaves on a serving platter. Fill each cup with ¼ cup of the pork mixture and sprinkle 1 tsp green onions and ½ tsp ground peanuts over top of each cup. Serve warm.

tip To make this recipe peanut-free, substitute 1½ tbsp ground almonds or cashews for the peanuts or simply omit the peanuts.

Nutrition per serving
CALORIES: 275   **FAT:** 18g   **NET CARBS:** 3g   **PROTEIN:** 9g

CREAMY DIJON CHICKEN SALAD

Creamy Dijon mustard and tender chicken make this low-carb keto chicken salad a flavorful, quick, and easy keto recipe. It's a snap to prepare shredded chicken in the Instant Pot!

SERVES: 2
SERVING SIZE: 2 CUPS LETTUCE WITH ½ CUP CHICKEN SALAD

PREP: 5 MINUTES
PRESSURE: 8 MINUTES
TOTAL: 13 MINUTES

SETTING: PRESSURE COOK
RELEASE: QUICK

1 Add the chicken broth to the pot. Season the chicken breast tenders with the sea salt and add to the pot.

2 Cover, lock the lid, and flip the steam release handle to the sealing position. Select **Pressure Cook (High)** and set the cook time for **8 minutes.** When the cook time is complete, quick release the pressure.

3 Open the lid. Using tongs, transfer the chicken to a cutting board and use two forks to shred the chicken. Transfer the shredded chicken to a large bowl.

4 To the bowl with the chicken, add the celery, green onion, balsamic vinegar, Dijon mustard, mayonnaise, parsley, and black pepper. Mix until well combined.

5 Add 2 cups spring lettuce mix to 2 serving plates each. Top each salad with ½ cup of the chicken salad and sprinkle 1 teaspoon chives over top of each salad. Serve promptly.

⅔ cup chicken broth

½lb (225g) boneless, skinless chicken breast tenders

½ tsp fine grind sea salt

1 celery stalk, minced

½ green onion, thinly sliced

½ tbsp balsamic vinegar

2 tbsp Dijon mustard

1½ tbsp mayonnaise

1 tbsp finely chopped flat-leaf parsley

¼ tsp ground black pepper

4 cups spring lettuce mix

2 tsp finely chopped chives

tip *If using frozen chicken breast tenders in this recipe, increase the pressure cooking time to 12 minutes.*

Nutrition per serving
CALORIES: 208 **FAT:** 6g **NET CARBS:** 1g **PROTEIN:** 30g

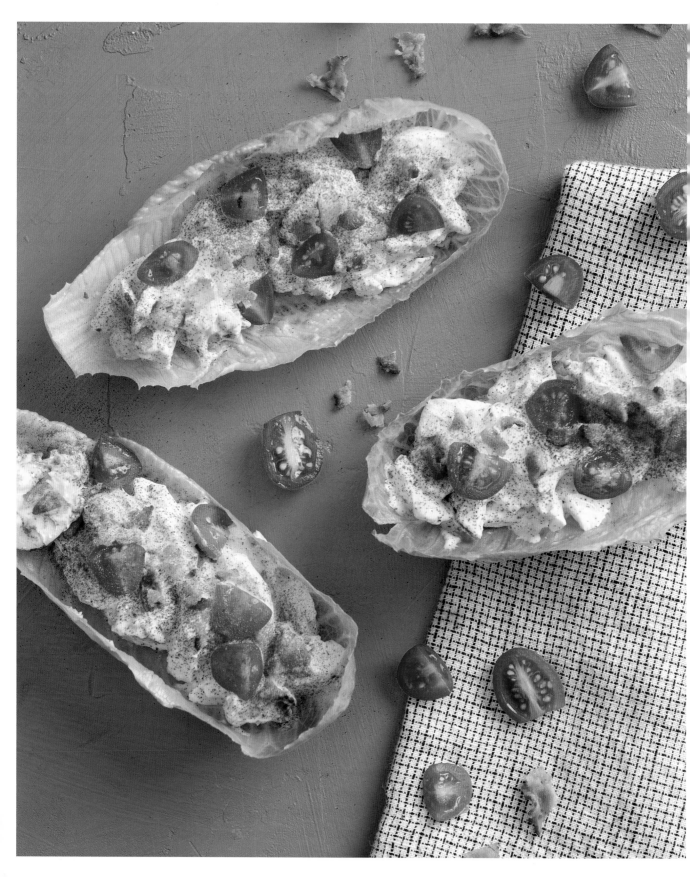

BLT EGG SALAD
in Lettuce Cups

This simple-to-prepare salad is served in a crisp cup of romaine lettuce and features the classic flavor combination of bacon, tomato, and egg. It has all the classic BLT flavor, but without the carb-heavy bread!

SERVES: 4
SERVING SIZE: 2 LETTUCE CUPS

PREP: 5 MINUTES
PRESSURE: 6 MINUTES
TOTAL: 23 MINUTES

SETTING: PRESSURE COOK
RELEASE: NATURAL/QUICK

4 large eggs
¼ cup mayonnaise
1 tsp fine grind sea salt
¼ tsp ground black pepper
8 medium hearts-of-romaine lettuce leaves
2 slices cooked bacon, crumbed
¼ tsp paprika
1 small Roma tomato, diced

1 Place the steam rack in the inner pot and add 1 cup water to the bottom of the pot. Place the eggs on the steam rack.

2 Cover, lock the lid, and flip the steam release handle to the sealing position. Select **Pressure Cook (High)** and set the cook time for **6 minutes.**

3 While the eggs are cooking, create an ice water bath by filling a large bowl halfway with cold water and ice. Set aside.

4 When the cook time for the eggs is complete, allow the pressure to release naturally for 6 minutes and then quick release the remaining pressure.

5 Open the lid and use tongs to carefully transfer the eggs to the ice water bath. Allow the eggs to cool in the bath for 6 minutes.

6 Once the eggs are cool enough to handle, transfer to a cutting board, peel, and roughly chop. Transfer the chopped eggs to a medium bowl.

7 To the bowl with the chopped eggs, add the mayonnaise, sea salt, and black pepper. Mix until well combined.

8 Arrange the lettuce shells on a platter. Spoon equal amounts of the egg salad into each shell and then top each with equal amounts of the bacon. Sprinkle the paprika over top and garnish with the tomatoes. Serve promptly.

tip *Butter lettuce leaves can be substituted for the romaine leaves.*

Nutrition per serving
CALORIES: 195 **FAT:** 16g **NET CARBS:** 2g **PROTEIN:** 8g

SERVES: 4
SERVING SIZE: ½ CUP NOODLES
WITH 2 TBSP SAUCE

PREP: 6 MINUTES
PRESSURE: 18 MINUTES
TOTAL: 1 HOUR 5 MINUTES

SETTING: PRESSURE COOK
RELEASE: NATURAL/QUICK

2lb (1kg) spaghetti squash

⅓ cup unsalted raw almonds

1 cup fresh basil leaves

¼ cup flat-leaf parsley

3 garlic cloves

½ cup olive oil

½ tsp fine grind sea salt

½ tsp ground black pepper

3 tbsp grated Parmesan cheese

tip *The cook time for the spaghetti squash is based on a 2lb (1kg) squash. For larger squash, add an additional 8 minutes per pound to the cooking time.*

To make this recipe dairy-free, omit the Parmesan.

SPAGHETTI SQUASH
with Almond Pesto

This delicious alternative to traditional pasta is low carb and gluten-free. The squash noodles are topped with a rich and flavorful almond pesto sauce that is fragrant with garlic and basil.

1 Preheat the oven to 400°F (204°C) and line a large baking sheet with aluminum foil. Set aside.

2 Using a sharp paring knife, pierce all sides of the squash to allow the steam to penetrate during cooking.

3 Place the steam rack in the inner pot and add 1 cup water to the bottom of the pot. Place the squash on top of the rack.

4 Cover, lock the lid, and flip the steam release handle to the sealing position. Select **Pressure Cook (High)** and set the cook time for **18 minutes.** When the cook time is complete, allow the pressure to release naturally for 10 minutes and then quick release the remaining pressure.

5 Open the lid and carefully remove the rack and squash from the pot. Set aside to cool for 15 minutes or until the squash is cool enough to handle.

6 Spread the almonds across the prepared baking sheet and place in the oven to toast for 7–10 minutes or until golden brown. Remove from the oven and set aside to cool for 5 minutes.

7 Make the pesto sauce by combining the toasted almonds, basil, parsley, garlic cloves, olive oil, sea salt, black pepper, and Parmesan in a food processor or blender. Pulse until the ingredients are well combined and form a thick paste. Set aside.

8 Cut the cooled spaghetti squash in half lengthwise. Using a spoon, scoop out and discard the seeds.

9 Using a fork, scrape the flesh of the squash to create the noodles. Transfer the noodles to a large bowl.

10 Add ½ cup squash noodles each to 4 serving bowls. Top each serving with 2 tbsp of the pesto sauce. Serve hot.

Nutrition per serving
CALORIES: 380   **FAT:** 32g   **NET CARBS:** 10g   **PROTEIN:** 5g

CABBAGE AND PANCETTA
in Cream Sauce

Healthy, nutrient-dense cabbage and smoky pancetta are smothered in a rich and savory cream sauce and accented with delicate spices in this low-carb side that is also gluten-free.

SERVES: 4
SERVING SIZE: ¾ CUP

PREP: 6 MINUTES
PRESSURE: 4 MINUTES
TOTAL: 20 MINUTES

SETTINGS: SAUTÉ/ PRESSURE COOK/SAUTÉ
RELEASE: QUICK

1 Select **Sauté (Normal).** Once the pot becomes hot, add the butter.

2 Once the butter is melted, add the pancetta and onions. Sauté, stirring continuously, for about 4 minutes or until the onions soften and begin to brown.

3 Add the chicken broth. Using a wooden spoon, stir and loosen any browned bits from the bottom of the pot.

4 Add the cabbage and bay leaf. Stir. Loosely cover the cabbage with a 7 x 7-inch (17.5 x 17.5cm) sheet of parchment paper and fold the corners down so the paper fits in the pot.

5 Cover, lock the lid, and flip the steam release handle to the sealing position. Select **Pressure Cook (High)** and set the cook time for **4 minutes.** When the cook time is complete, quick release the pressure.

6 Open the lid and remove the parchment paper. Select **Sauté (More)** and bring the ingredients to a boil.

7 Once the ingredients begin to boil, select **Sauté (Less).** Add the nutmeg, sea salt, black pepper, parsley, and heavy cream. Stir. Simmer for 5 additional minutes and then press **Cancel** to turn off the pot.

8 Remove and discard the bay leaf. Spoon into serving bowls. Serve warm.

1 tbsp unsalted butter

½ cup diced pancetta

¼ cup diced yellow onion

1 cup chicken broth

1lb (450g) green cabbage, finely chopped (about ½ medium head)

1 bay leaf

¼ tsp ground nutmeg

1 tsp fine grind sea salt

¼ tsp ground black pepper

1 tbsp dried parsley

⅓ cup heavy cream

tip *To make this dairy-free, substitute 1 tbsp avocado oil for the butter and ⅓ cup unsweetened full-fat coconut milk for the heavy cream.*

Nutrition per serving
CALORIES: 210 **FAT:** 17g **NET CARBS:** 5g **PROTEIN:** 7g

SERVES: 8
SERVING SIZE: 1 SLICE

PREP: 5 MINUTES
COOK: 2 HOURS 30 MINUTES
TOTAL: 2 HOURS 40 MINUTES

SETTING: SLOW COOK
RELEASE: NONE

½ medium head cauliflower, trimmed, stem removed, and chopped into florets

3½ tbsp coconut flour

1½ cup grated mozzarella cheese, divided

¼ tsp fine grind sea salt

2 tbsp unsalted butter, divided

2 large eggs, beaten

2 tbsp heavy cream

2 garlic cloves, minced

2 tbsp fresh basil, cut into ribbons (optional)

CHEESY GARLIC CAULIFLOWER FLATBREAD

The gluten-free flatbread is aromatic and garlicky, and topped with gooey mozzarella. It's a perfect low-carb keto side or appetizer, and the cauliflower helps make it high in fiber and nutrient-rich.

1 Add the cauliflower to a blender or food processor and pulse until a ricelike texture is formed.

2 In a large bowl, combine the coconut flour, ¾ cup mozzarella, ⅔ cup of the riced cauliflower, and sea salt. Mix until well combined.

3 Melt 1 tablespoon of the butter in the microwave. Add the eggs, heavy cream, and melted butter to the bowl with the cauliflower mixture. Stir until the ingredients are thoroughly combined and no lumps remain.

4 Coat the bottom of the inner pot with the remaining butter. Add the cauliflower mixture and use a spoon to press the mixture flat into the bottom of the pot. Sprinkle the garlic and remaining mozzarella over top of the mixture.

5 Cover and lock the lid, but leave the steam release handle in the venting position. Select **Slow Cook (More)** and cook for **2 hours 30 minutes** or until the edges are browned.

6 While the flatbread is cooking, preheat the oven broiler to 450°F (232°C).

7 Once the cook time for the flatbread is complete, transfer the flatbread to a cutting board and cut into 8 equal-sized wedges. Place the wedges on a large baking sheet and transfer to the oven to broil for 2–3 minutes or until the cheese is lightly browned.

8 Remove from the oven and transfer to a serving platter. Sprinkle the basil ribbons over top (if using). Serve warm.

tip *This flatbread can also be used as a tasty low-carb pizza crust.*

Nutrition per serving
CALORIES: 135 **FAT:** 10g **NET CARBS:** 2g **PROTEIN:** 6g

SERVES: 4
SERVING SIZE: 1 RAMEKIN

 PREP: 5 MINUTES
PRESSURE: 3 MINUTES
TOTAL: 13 MINUTES

 SETTING: STEAM
RELEASE: QUICK

1 medium head cauliflower, cut into florets

1 tbsp chicken broth

½ tbsp unsalted butter, melted

2 garlic cloves

⅓ cup fresh mozzarella cheese, cubed

1 tsp fine grind sea salt

¼ tsp ground black pepper

2 tbsp shredded Parmesan cheese

¼ cup shredded cheddar cheese

½ tbsp chopped flat-leaf parsley

CHEESY GARLIC CAULIFLOWER MASH

This creamy cauliflower mash is accented with fragrant garlic and covered in warm, gooey cheese. It's just as satisfying and comforting as mashed potatoes but without all the carbs!

1 Preheat the oven broiler to high. Spray four 4-ounce (110g) ramekins with coconut oil cooking spray. Set aside.

2 Place a steamer basket with legs in the pot and add 1 cup water to the bottom of the pot. Add the cauliflower florets to the steamer basket.

3 Cover, lock the lid, and flip the steam release handle to the sealing position. Select **Steam (High)** and set the cook time for **3 minutes.** When the cook time is complete, quick release the pressure.

4 Open the lid and transfer half the cauliflower florets to a large food processor or blender. Pulse until a thick, creamy texture is achieved.

5 Use a rubber spatula to scrape the sides of the blender and then add the remaining cauliflower florets along with the chicken broth and melted butter. Blend until thick and creamy.

6 Add the garlic, mozzarella, sea salt, and black pepper. Pulse until the ingredients are combined and a smooth, creamy texture is achieved.

7 Add equal amounts of the cauliflower mash to the prepared ramekins. Sprinkle ½ tbsp Parmesan and 1 tbsp shredded cheddar cheese over top of each ramekin.

8 Place the ramekins under the oven broiler for 4–5 minutes or until the cheese begins to brown. Remove from the oven and garnish each serving with equal amounts of the parsley. Serve hot.

tip To make this recipe dairy-free, omit the mozzarella and Parmesan, and substitute ½ tbsp avocado oil for the melted butter and ¼ cup shredded almond cheese for the cheddar.

Nutrition per serving
CALORIES: 125 **FAT:** 7g **NET CARBS:** 5g **PROTEIN:** 8g

BUFFALO CHICKEN SALAD
in Lettuce Cups

This creamy chicken salad is extremely low in carbs and features a tangy buffalo sauce, Gorgonzola cheese, and fresh, crunchy bits of celery. It's satisfying, full of flavor, and all tucked inside a lettuce cup.

1 Add the chicken broth to the inner pot and season with the salt and pepper. Add the the chicken thighs to the pot.

2 Cover, lock the lid, and flip the steam release handle to the sealing position. Select **Pressure Cook (High)** and set the cook time for **6 minutes.**

3 When the cook time is complete, allow the pressure to release naturally for 10 minutes and then quick release the remaining pressure.

4 Open the lid and transfer the cooked chicken to a cutting board. Using forks, shred the chicken and then transfer to a large bowl.

5 To the bowl with the chicken, add the mayonnaise, melted butter, hot pepper sauce, garlic powder, celery seed, and celery. Mix well to combine.

6 Arrange the lettuce cups on a large platter. Fill each cup with equal amounts of the buffalo chicken salad and sprinkle ½ tbsp Gorgonzola over top of each cup. Serve promptly.

SERVES: 2
SERVING SIZE: 2 LETTUCE CUPS

PREP: 4 MINUTES
PRESSURE: 6 MINUTES
TOTAL: 20 MINUTES

SETTING: PRESSURE COOK
RELEASE: NATURAL/QUICK

1 cup chicken broth

¼ tsp fine grind sea salt

⅛ tsp ground black pepper

½lb (225g) boneless, skinless chicken thighs

3 tbsp mayonnaise

2½ tbsp unsalted butter, melted

⅓ cup hot pepper sauce

¼ tsp garlic powder

¼ tsp celery seed

1 medium celery stalk, minced

4 large butter lettuce leaves

2 tbsp crumbled Gorgonzola cheese

tip *Romaine lettuce hearts can be substituted for the butter lettuce leaves.*

Nutrition per serving
CALORIES: 430 **FAT:** 35g **NET CARBS:** 1g **PROTEIN:** 24g

SERVES: 4
SERVING SIZE: 1 CUP

PREP: 5 MINUTES
PRESSURE: 2 MINUTES
TOTAL: 18 MINUTES

SETTINGS: PRESSURE COOK/SAUTÉ
RELEASE: QUICK

1 head cauliflower, trimmed, stem removed, and cut into medium florets

2 tbsp avocado oil

1 garlic clove, minced

Juice of 1 lime

⅛ tsp fine grind sea salt (optional)

4 sprigs fresh cilantro, chopped

CILANTRO LIME CAULIFLOWER RICE

With refreshing accents of lime and cilantro, this riced cauliflower dish is a perfect accompaniment to any meal. Pulsing the cauliflower florets transforms them into a fluffy, low-carb alternative to rice.

1 Place the steam rack in the inner pot and add 1 cup water to the bottom of the pot. Place a steamer basket with legs on top of the steam rack. Add the cauliflower to the steamer basket.

2 Cover, lock the lid, and flip the steam release handle to the sealing position. Select **Pressure Cook (High)** and set the cook time for **2 minutes.** Once the cook time is complete, quick release the pressure.

3 Open the lid and remove the steamer basket and cauliflower from the pot. Set aside. Carefully remove the inner pot from the base, wipe dry with a paper towel, and then return the pot to the base.

4 Transfer the cauliflower florets to a food processor and pulse until a ricelike texture is achieved. Set aside.

5 Select **Sauté (Normal).** Once the pot is hot, add the avocado oil and garlic. Sauté the garlic for 2 minutes or until it becomes soft and fragrant.

6 Add the riced cauliflower and sauté for 2 additional minutes, or until the rice becomes soft.

7 Stir in the lime juice and sauté for 2 additional minutes.

8 Transfer the cauliflower rice to a serving dish. Season with the sea salt (if using) and garnish with the cilantro. Serve hot.

tip *An equal amount of olive oil or coconut oil can be substituted for the avocado oil.*

If you don't have a steamer basket with legs, you can use an ovenproof bowl placed on the steam rack.

Nutrition per serving
CALORIES: 105   **FAT:** 7g   **NET CARBS:** 4g   **PROTEIN:** 3g

GARLICKY FRIED CAULIFLOWER RICE
with Mushrooms

This satisfying keto dish features scrambled egg, buttery mushrooms, and fragrant garlic. It's incredibly simple to prepare in the Instant Pot and is a wonderful low-carb alternative to traditional fried rice!

SERVES: 4
SERVING SIZE: 1 CUP

PREP: 5 MINUTES
PRESSURE: 3 MINUTES
TOTAL: 23 MINUTES

SETTINGS: STEAM/SAUTÉ
RELEASE: QUICK

---

1 medium head cauliflower, cut into florets

1½ tbsp unsalted butter

3 garlic cloves, minced

1 cup sliced fresh white mushrooms

1 tsp tamari sauce

1½ tbsp olive oil

1 large egg, beaten

¼ tsp fine grind sea salt

⅛ tsp ground black pepper

½ tbsp chopped fresh flat-leaf parsley

1 Place a steamer basket with legs in the inner pot and add 1 cup water to the bottom of the pot. Place the cauliflower florets in the steamer basket.

2 Cover, lock the lid, and flip the steam release handle to the sealing position. Select **Steam (High)** and set the cook time for **3 minutes.** When the cook time is complete, quick release the pressure.

3 Open the lid and transfer cauliflower florets to a food processor. Pulse until a ricelike texture is achieved. Set aside.

4 Remove the steamer basket from the pot. Carefully remove the inner pot from the base, drain and wipe dry with a paper towel, and then return the pot to the base.

5 Select **Sauté (Normal).** Once the pot is hot, add the butter. Once the butter is melted, add the garlic and mushrooms and sauté for 4 minutes or until the mushrooms have softened.

6 Add the tamari sauce and stir. Add the olive oil and cauliflower rice and sauté for 3 additional minutes.

7 Add the beaten egg to the pot and stir continuously for 3 minutes, or until the egg is thoroughly cooked. Add the sea salt and black pepper and stir to combine.

8 Transfer the fried rice to serving bowls and sprinkle the parsley over top. Serve hot.

tip *To make this recipe soy-free, substitute 1 tsp coconut aminos for the tamari sauce.*

To make this recipe dairy-free, substitute 1½ tbsp avocado oil for the butter.

Nutrition per serving
CALORIES: 130   **FAT:** 9g   **NET CARBS:** 5g   **PROTEIN:** 5g

SHRIMP AND BACON SALAD
with *Lemon Dijon Dressing*

This loaded keto salad is very low in carbs but features the bold flavors of sautéed shrimp, fragrant paprika, and smoky bacon. It's topped with creamy avocado slices and a refreshing citrus Dijon dressing.

1 Make the dressing by combining the olive oil, lemon juice, and Dijon mustard in a small bowl. Whisk until blended. Cover with plastic wrap and place in the refrigerator to chill.

2 Combine the shrimp, paprika, ¼ tsp sea salt, and black pepper in a medium bowl. Toss the shrimp to coat in the spices. Set aside.

3 Select **Sauté (Normal)**. Once the pot is hot, add the bacon slices and cook for 5 minutes per side or until crisp.

4 Transfer the bacon to a plate, blot with paper towels, and then transfer to a cutting board and roughly chop. Set aside.

5 Add the shrimp to the bacon grease in the pot and cook for 2 minutes per side or until the shrimp are opaque. Transfer the shrimp to a large bowl and season with the remaining salt.

6 Add equal amounts of the romaine and spring lettuce mix to 2 serving plates. Top each serving with equal amounts of the cherry tomatoes, avocado slices, chopped bacon, and shrimp.

7 Remove the dressing from the refrigerator. Whisk to combine and then drizzle 1½ tablespoons over top of each salad. Serve promptly.

 SERVES: 2
SERVING SIZE: 1 SALAD WITH ¼LB (115G) SHRIMP

 PREP: 5 MINUTES
COOK: 14 MINUTES
TOTAL: 19 MINUTES

SETTING: SAUTÉ
RELEASE: NONE

½ lb (224g) medium fresh wild-caught shrimp, peeled, deveined, and rinsed and patted dry

½ tsp paprika

½ tsp fine grind sea salt, divided

¼ tsp ground black pepper

2 slices uncooked bacon

2 cup romaine lettuce, chopped into bite-sized pieces

2 cups spring lettuce mix

6 cherry tomatoes, sliced in half

½ medium avocado, cut into 6 equal-sized slices

FOR THE DRESSING

1½ tbsp extra virgin olive oil

2 tbsp fresh lemon juice

½ tsp Dijon mustard

tip *If using frozen shrimp, first defrost the shrimp and then rinse and pat dry before adding to the pot.*

Nutrition per serving
CALORIES: 255 **FAT:** 20g **NET CARBS:** 3g **PROTEIN:** 21g

SERVES: 4
SERVING SIZE: ABOUT 7 SPEARS WITH 2 TSP LEMON BUTTER SAUCE AND 1 TSP PARMESAN CHEESE

PREP: 3 MINUTES
PRESSURE: 2 MINUTES
TOTAL: 8 MINUTES

SETTINGS: STEAM/SAUTÉ
RELEASE: QUICK

1lb (450g) fresh asparagus spears, cut in half and woody ends removed

2 tbsp butter

1 garlic clove, minced

2 tsp fresh lemon juice

1½ tbsp shredded Parmesan cheese

STEAMED ASPARAGUS
with Garlic Parmesan Lemon Butter

This simple side is lightly steamed and topped with a lovely drizzle of citrusy garlic butter and a touch of Parmesan. The Instant Pot steams asparagus perfectly al dente in a snap!

1 Place the steam rack in the inner pot and add 1 cup water to the bottom of the pot. Place the asparagus spears on the rack.

2 Cover, lock the lid, and flip the steam release handle to the sealing position. Select **Steam (High)** and set the cook time for **2 minutes**. When the cook time is complete, quick release the pressure.

3 Open the lid and carefully remove the steamer basket and asparagus spears from the pot. Set aside.

4 Carefully remove the inner pot from the base, drain and wipe dry with a paper towel, and then return the pot to the base.

5 Select **Sauté (Normal).** Once the pot is hot, add the butter and garlic. Sauté for 2 minutes or until the garlic becomes fragrant. Add the lemon juice, stir, and then press **Cancel** to turn off the pot.

6 Transfer the asparagus spears to a serving platter. Drizzle with the lemon garlic butter and sprinkle the Parmesan over top. Serve warm.

tip *If you don't have a steamer basket with legs, you can use an ovenproof bowl placed on top of the steam rack.*

Nutrition per serving
CALORIES: 76   **FAT:** 4g   **NET CARBS:** 3g   **PROTEIN:** 3g

BALSAMIC GLAZED BRUSSELS SPROUTS

These perfectly-cooked sprouts are lightly seasoned and cooked in a tangy and sweet balsamic butter. The Instant Pot does a superb job of cooking these quickly while still preserving texture and flavor.

SERVES: 4
SERVING SIZE: ⅓ CUP

PREP: 2 MINUTES
PRESSURE: 2 MINUTES
TOTAL: 7 MINUTES

SETTINGS: PRESSURE COOK/SAUTÉ
RELEASE: QUICK

2 cups whole Brussels sprouts, trimmed and halved

2 tbsp unsalted butter

1 garlic clove, minced

1½ tbsp balsamic vinegar

½ tbsp chives, chopped

¼ tsp fine grind sea salt

⅛ tsp ground black pepper

1 Place the steam rack in the inner pot and place a steamer basket with legs on top of the rack. Add 1½ cups water to the bottom of the pot. Place the sprouts in an even layer in the steamer basket.

2 Cover, lock the lid, and flip the steam release handle to the sealing position. Select **Pressure Cook (High)** and set the cook time for **2 minutes.** When the cook time is complete, quick release the pressure.

3 Open the lid and transfer the sprouts to a medium bowl. Set aside.

4 Remove the steam rack from the pot. Carefully remove the inner pot from the base, drain and wipe dry with a paper towel, and then return the pot to the base.

5 Select **Sauté (Normal).** Once the inner pot is hot, add the butter and garlic. Sauté, stirring frequently, for 1–2 minutes or until the garlic becomes soft and fragrant.

6 Add the balsamic vinegar and stir. Add the sprouts back to the pot and sauté for 1 additional minute, stirring continuously, to coat the sprouts in the sauce. Press **Cancel** to turn off the pot.

7 Transfer the sprouts and sauce to a serving dish. Sprinkle the chives over top and season with the sea salt and black pepper. Serve hot.

tip *To make this recipe dairy-free, substitute 2 tbsp avocado oil for the butter.*

Nutrition per serving
CALORIES: 74 **FAT:** 6g **NET CARBS:** 3g **PROTEIN:** 2g

SERVES: 4
SERVING SIZE: ¾ CUP

PREP: 5 MINUTES
PRESSURE: 2 MINUTES
TOTAL: 11 MINUTES

SETTINGS: STEAM/SAUTÉ
RELEASE: QUICK

1lb (450g) fresh green beans, washed and trimmed

3 tbsp butter

1 garlic clove, minced

1½ cup sliced fresh mushrooms

2 tsp tamari sauce

4 slices cooked bacon, crumbled

⅛ tsp ground black pepper

GREEN BEANS
with Mushrooms and Bacon

These fresh, vibrant green beans and buttery glazed mushrooms are accented with smoky bacon and fragrant garlic. This simple yet elegant keto side is a wonderful accompaniment to any meal.

1 Place the green beans in the bottom of the inner pot and add just enough water to cover the beans.

2 Cover, lock the lid, and flip the steam release handle to the sealing position. Select **Steam (High)** and set the cook time for **2 minutes.** When the cook time is complete, quick release the pressure.

3 Open the lid and transfer the beans to a colander to drain. Set aside.

4 Carefully remove the inner pot from the base, drain and wipe dry with a paper towel, and then return the pot to the base.

5 Select **Sauté (Normal).** Once the pot becomes hot, add the butter.

6 Once the butter is melted, add the garlic and mushrooms to the pot and sauté for 1 minute or until the mushrooms begin to soften.

7 Add the tamari sauce. Continue sautéing, stirring continuously, for 1 minute or until the mushrooms have fully absorbed the sauce.

8 Add the green beans and crumbled bacon to the pot. Sauté for 1 additional minute, stirring to coat the beans and bacon in the sauce.

9 Transfer the beans and mushrooms to a serving plate and season with the black pepper. Serve hot.

tip *To make this recipe soy-free, substitute 2 tsp coconut aminos for the tamari sauce.*

Nutrition per serving
CALORIES: 178   **FAT:** 12g   **NET CARBS:** 7g   **PROTEIN:** 6g

SERVES: 4
SERVING SIZE: ½ CUP

PREP: 3 MINUTES
PRESSURE: 2 MINUTES
TOTAL: 7 MINUTES

SETTINGS: STEAM/SAUTÉ
RELEASE: QUICK

2 cups fresh broccoli florets
2 tbsp butter
1½ tsp lemon juice
½ tsp freshly grated lemon zest
¼ tsp fine grind sea salt
¼ tsp ground black pepper

ZESTY LEMON PEPPER BROCCOLI

This simple, low-carb, nutrient-dense side features tender broccoli steamed perfectly and quickly in the Instant Pot and accented with a tangy and lively lemon pepper butter sauce.

1 Place the steam rack in the inner pot and add 1 cup water to the bottom of the pot. Add the broccoli florets.

2 Cover, lock the lid, and flip the steam release handle to the sealing position. Select **Steam (High)** and set the cook time for **2 minutes.** When the cook time is complete, quick release the pressure.

3 Open the lid and transfer the broccoli to a small bowl. Set aside.

4 Carefully remove the steam rack from the pot, drain and wipe dry with a paper towel, and then return the pot to the base.

5 Select **Sauté (Normal).** Once the inner pot becomes hot, add the butter. Once the butter is melted, add the lemon juice and lemon zest. Stir lightly, just until the ingredients are combined.

6 Add the broccoli florets to the pot. Gently toss to coat with the lemon butter sauce.

7 Transfer the broccoli and sauce to a medium serving bowl and season with the sea salt and black pepper. Serve hot.

tip Always use the quick pressure release method when cooking vegetables in the Instant Pot. Allowing the pressure to release naturally can result in many vegetables becoming overcooked and mushy.

Nutrition per serving
CALORIES: 56 **FAT:** 6g **NET CARBS:** 0g **PROTEIN:** 0g

BUTTERY SAUTÉED GARLIC MUSHROOMS

These rich and buttery mushrooms are low-carb and served in a savory, aromatic garlic sauce for an extraordinary keto side. These also are excellent when served over steak or chicken, or on burgers.

SERVES: 4
SERVING SIZE: ⅓ CUP

PREP: 2 MINUTES
COOK: 5 MINUTES
TOTAL: 7 MINUTES

SETTING: SAUTÉ
RELEASE: NONE

¼ tsp arrowroot powder
2 tbsp butter, divided
3 garlic cloves, minced
2 cups sliced fresh mushrooms
½ cup chicken broth
¼ tsp fine grind sea salt
⅛ tsp ground black pepper

1 In a small bowl, combine the arrowroot powder and 1 tablespoon of the butter. Using a fork, cut the butter into the arrowroot powder until the ingredients are well incorporated. Set aside.

2 Select **Sauté (Normal).** Once the pot is hot, add the remaining butter.

3 Once the butter has melted, add the garlic and mushrooms. Sauté, stirring frequently, for 2 minutes or until the mushrooms soften and the garlic becomes fragrant.

4 Add the chicken broth. Continue sautéing, stirring frequently, for 2 additional minutes or until the mushrooms are browned.

5 Add the arrowroot-butter mixture to the pot. Stir until the mixture is melted and the sauce is bubbling and begins to thicken slightly, and then press **Cancel** to turn off the pot.

6 Transfer the mushrooms and sauce to a serving bowl and season with the sea salt and black pepper. Serve warm.

tip *Arrowroot powder is a plant-based starch and is used as a thickening agent. It can be omitted, if desired, but the sauce will be slightly thinner.*

Nutrition per serving
CALORIES: 72   **FAT:** 4g   **NET CARBS:** 2g   **PROTEIN:** 2g

BRAISED ENDIVE
with Bacon and Gorgonzola

Endive is paired with savory bacon and tangy Gorgonzola to create a sophisticated-tasting, French-inspired vegetable side that features bold flavors and also is very simple to make in the Instant Pot.

SERVES: 4
SERVING SIZE: 2 HALVES

PREP: 3 MINUTES
PRESSURE: 1 MINUTE
TOTAL: 8 MINUTES

SETTINGS: STEAM/SAUTÉ
RELEASE: QUICK

1 Place the steam rack in the inner pot and add 1 cup water to the bottom of the pot. Place the endive halves on the rack.

2 Cover, lock the lid, and flip the steam release handle to the sealing position. Select **Steam** and set the cook time for **1 minute.** When the cook time is complete, quick release the pressure.

3 Open the lid and carefully transfer the endive halves to a plate. Set aside.

4 Remove the steam rack from the pot. Carefully remove the inner pot from the base, drain, rinse, and wipe dry with a paper towel, and then return the pot to the base.

5 Select **Sauté (Normal).** Once the pot is hot, add the butter.

6 Once the butter is melted, place the endive halves in the pot, sliced-sides down, and sauté for 2 minutes or until browned (do not stir).

7 Flip the endive halves and brown the opposite sides for 2 additional minutes. Add the bacon.

8 Transfer the endive halves to a serving platter. Spoon the bacon over top of the halves, sprinkle the Gorgonzola over top, and season with the sea salt and black pepper. Serve warm.

4 medium heads Belgian endive, halved lengthwise

1½ tbsp unsalted butter

2 slices cooked bacon, crumbled

2 tbsp Gorgonzola cheese

⅛ tsp fine grind sea salt

⅛ tsp ground black pepper

tip To make this recipe dairy-free, substitute 1½ tablespoons olive oil for the butter and omit the Gorgonzola.

Nutrition per serving
CALORIES: 77 **FAT:** 5g **NET CARBS:** 2g **PROTEIN:** 4g

SERVES: 5
SERVING SIZE: ½ CUP

PREP: 5 MINUTES
PRESSURE: 2 MINUTES
TOTAL: 12 MINUTES

SETTING: STEAM
RELEASE: QUICK

1½ cups sliced zucchini

1½ cups sliced yellow squash

2½ tbsp butter, melted

½ tbsp Italian seasoning blend

½ tsp fine grind sea salt

¼ tsp ground black pepper

2 tbsp grated Parmesan cheese

ITALIAN SQUASH MEDLEY

This colorful side features lightly steamed squash seasoned with Parmesan cheese and bright Italian spices. It's extremely low in carbs and makes a wonderful accompaniment to any protein.

1 Place a steamer basket with legs in the inner pot and add 1½ cups water to the bottom of the pot. Add the zucchini and yellow squash to the basket.

2 Cover, lock the lid, and flip the steam release handle to the sealing position. Select **Steam (High)** and set the cook time for **2 minutes.** When the cook time is complete, quick release the pressure.

3 Open the lid and transfer the zucchini and squash to a large bowl.

4 Add the melted butter, Italian seasoning, sea salt, black pepper, and Parmesan cheese to the bowl. Toss to coat the zucchini and squash in the butter and spices.

5 Transfer the squash medley to serving plates. Serve hot.

tip *If you don't have a steamer basket with legs, you can use an ovenproof bowl placed on top of the steam rack.*

Nutrition per serving
CALORIES: 74 **FAT:** 6g **NET CARBS:** 1g **PROTEIN:** 1g

STEAMED BROCCOLI AND CAULIFLOWER
with Herbs

Fresh steamed vegetables are paired with fragrant garlic, tangy Parmesan cheese and herbs in this low-carb side that is super simple to prepare in the Instant Pot.

SERVES: 4
SERVING SIZE: ½ CUP

PREP: 5 MINUTES
PRESSURE: 3 MINUTES
TOTAL: 13 MINUTES

SETTING: STEAM
RELEASE: QUICK

1 cup fresh broccoli florets
1 cup fresh cauliflower florets
3 tbsp olive oil
2 garlic cloves, minced
3 tbsp grated Parmesan cheese
½ tsp dried parsley
¼ tsp dried thyme
½ tsp fine grind sea salt
¼ tsp ground black pepper

1   Line a large baking sheet with aluminum foil. Set aside.

2   Place a steamer basket with legs in the inner pot and add 1 cup water to the bottom of the pot. Add the broccoli and cauliflower florets to the basket.

3   Cover, lock the lid, and flip the steam release handle to the sealing position. Select **Steam (High)** and set the cook time for **3 minutes.**

4   While the vegetables are cooking, preheat the oven broiler to 550°F (288°C).

5   When the cook time for the vegetables is complete, quick release the pressure. Open the lid, and transfer the broccoli and cauliflower to a large bowl.

6   To the bowl with the broccoli and cauliflower, add the olive oil, garlic, Parmesan, parsley, thyme, sea salt, and black pepper. Toss to coat.

7   Arrange the vegetables in a single layer on the prepared baking sheet. Place under the broiler for 5 minutes or until the vegetables begin to brown.

8   Carefully the remove baking sheet from the oven and transfer the vegetables to a serving bowl. Serve hot.

tip *If using frozen broccoli and cauliflower florets, increase the steaming time to 4 minutes.*

Nutrition per serving
CALORIES: 112   **FAT:** 11g   **NET CARBS:** 1g   **PROTEIN:** 2g

SERVES: 4
SERVING SIZE: ½ ARTICHOKE HEART WITH 2 TBSP SAUCE

PREP: 5 MINUTES
PRESSURE: 11 MINUTES
TOTAL: 26 MINUTES

SETTING: STEAM
RELEASE: NATURAL/QUICK

½ cup water

½ cup chicken broth

2 garlic cloves, smashed

2 artichokes, stems and tough outer leaves removed and leaf points trimmed

FOR THE SAUCE

6 tbsp mayonnaise

1½ tbsp Dijon mustard

2 tsp lemon juice

¼ tsp fine grind sea salt

¼ tsp ground black pepper

STEAMED ARTICHOKES
with Creamy Dijon Sauce

This classic vegetable side is low in carbs and high in nutrients and fiber. It features a perfectly cooked artichoke and a creamy dipping sauce that has accents of citrus and mustard.

1 Make the sauce by combining the mayonnaise, Dijon mustard, lemon juice, sea salt, and black pepper in a medium bowl. Stir until well combined. Cover with plastic wrap and transfer to the refrigerator.

2 Add the water, chicken broth, and garlic to the inner pot. Stir.

3 Place the steam rack in the inner pot and place the artichokes upside down on the rack.

4 Cover, lock the lid, and flip the steam release handle to the sealing position. Select **Steam (High)** and set the cook time for **11 minutes.**

5 When the cook time is complete, allow the pressure to release naturally for 10 minutes and then quick release the remaining pressure.

6 Open the lid and use tongs to carefully transfer the artichokes to a cutting board. Slice the artichokes in half lengthwise.

7 Using a spoon, remove the hearts from the outer shells and transfer the artichoke halves and hearts to a plate.

8 Drizzle a small amount of the broth from the pot over top of the artichoke halves and hearts. Serve warm with the Dijon sauce on the side for dipping.

tip *Use a pair of kitchen shears to trim the pointed tips of the leaves, and a knife to remove the stems and tops.*

Nutrition per serving
CALORIES: 176 **FAT:** 15g **NET CARBS:** 4g **PROTEIN:** 3g

SERVES: 4
SERVING SIZE: ½ CUP CAULIFLOWER WITH 2 TBSP CHEESE SAUCE

PREP: 4 MINUTES
PRESSURE: 19 MINUTES
TOTAL: 23 MINUTES

SETTINGS: PRESSURE COOK/STEAM
RELEASE: QUICK

¼ cup full-fat sour cream

2oz (55g) block-style cream cheese

1 tbsp unsalted butter

⅓ cup shredded cheddar cheese

¼ cup heavy cream

½ tsp garlic powder

½ tsp fine grind sea salt

¼ tsp ground black pepper

2 cups fresh cauliflower florets

tip *If using frozen cauliflower florets in this recipe, increase the steaming time for the cauliflower to 6 minutes.*

STEAMED CAULIFLOWER
with Cheese Sauce

Perfectly steamed cauliflower is covered in a warm and creamy cheddar cheese sauce in this keto-friendly side that is low-carb, gluten-free, and full of antioxidants and healthy fats.

1 Place the steam rack in the inner pot and add 1 cup water to the bottom of the pot.

2 In a 6-inch (15.25cm) ovenproof soufflé dish, combine the sour cream, cream cheese, butter, cheddar cheese, heavy cream, garlic powder, sea salt, and black pepper. Tightly cover the dish with aluminum foil and place on the steam rack.

3 Cover, lock the lid, and flip the steam release handle to the sealing position. Select **Pressure Cook (High)** and set the cook time for **16 minutes.** When the cook time is complete, quick release the pressure.

4 Open the lid, grasp the rack handles, and carefully lift the rack and dish out of the pot. Remove the foil and vigorously stir the sauce until smooth and creamy, and then re-cover the dish with the foil. Set aside.

5 Carefully remove the inner pot from the base, drain, and then return the pot to the base. Place a steamer basket with legs in the pot and add 1 cup cold water to the bottom of the pot. Add the cauliflower florets to the steamer basket.

6 Cover, lock the lid, and flip the steam release handle to the sealing position. Select **Steam (High)** and set the cook time for **3 minutes.** When the cook time is complete, quick release the pressure.

7 Open the lid and use tongs to transfer the cauliflower florets to 4 serving bowls.

8 Remove the foil cover from the cheese sauce and stir. (If the sauce is too thick, add 1 tablespoon water and stir. Continue adding water until the desired consistency is achieved.)

9 Spoon 2 tablespoons of the cheese sauce over top of each serving. Serve hot.

Nutrition per serving
CALORIES: 215   **FAT:** 20g   **NET CARBS:** 4g   **PROTEIN:** 5g

SKIRT STEAK SALAD
with *Gorgonzola*

Tender and flavorful marinated skirt steak is topped with tangy Gorgonzola cheese and a refreshing vinaigrette in this hearty classic salad that is easy to prepare, low carb, and gluten-free.

SERVES: 4
SERVING SIZE: 1 SALAD WITH ¼LB (115G) STEAK

PREP: 6 MINUTES
PRESSURE: 25 MINUTES
TOTAL: 1 HOUR 10 MINUTES

SETTINGS: SAUTÉ/PRESSURE COOK
RELEASE: NATURAL/QUICK

1 Combine the olive oil, garlic, sea salt, black pepper, and paprika in a 1-gallon (3.8l) zippered freezer bag. Seal the bag and shake the ingredients to combine. Add the skirt steak to the bag, seal, and carefully rotate the bag to coat the steaks in the marinade. Place the bag with the steaks in the refrigerator to marinate for 20 minutes.

2 Select **Sauté.** Once the pot becomes hot, add the avocado oil and let the oil heat for 2 minutes. Remove the steaks from the bag, place in the pot and sauté for 3–4 minutes per side or until browned. Press **Cancel** to turn off pot. Transfer the steaks to a plate and set aside.

3 Add 1 cup cold water to the inner pot. Place a 20-inch (51cm) sheet of aluminum foil over the steam rack and fold the sides of the foil up. Place the marinated steaks on the rack and place the rack in the pot. Pour the leftover marinade from the bag over the steaks. Fold the sides of the aluminum foil over the steaks and crimp the edges shut to form a sealed packet.

4 Cover, lock the lid, and flip the steam release handle to the sealing position. Select **Pressure Cook (High)** and set the cook time for **25 minutes.**

5 While the steaks are cooking, make the vinaigrette by combining the olive oil, red wine vinegar, lemon juice, sea salt, and black pepper in a resealable container. Tightly seal the container and shake until the ingredients are well combined. Transfer to the refrigerator to chill.

6 When the cook time for the steaks is complete, allow the pressure to release naturally for 5 minutes and then quick release the remaining pressure. Open the lid, carefully transfer the foil packet to a cutting board, and open the packet to let the steaks rest for 5 minutes.

7 Add 1 cup spring mix lettuce and 1 cup romaine lettuce to each of 4 serving plates. Slice the steaks into thin strips and place equal amounts of the steak on top of each bed of lettuce. Top each salad with equal amounts of the cherry tomatoes and then crumble ½ tbsp Gorgonzola over top of each salad. Shake the vinaigrette and drizzle 2½ tablespoons over each salad. Serve promptly.

3 tbsp olive oil

2 garlic cloves, minced

½ tsp fine grind sea salt

¼ tsp ground black pepper

¼ tsp paprika

1lb (450g) skirt steak, cut into 4 equal-sized pieces

1 tbsp avocado oil

4 cups spring lettuce mix

½ head romaine lettuce, chopped into bite-sized pieces

12 cherry tomatoes, sliced in half

2 tbsp crumbled Gorgonzola cheese

FOR THE VINAIGRETTE

⅓ cup olive oil

3 tbsp red wine vinegar

2 tbsp fresh lemon juice

1 tsp fine grind sea salt

¼ tsp ground black pepper

tip *If you prefer the steak be more chilled, place the cooked and sliced steak in the refrigerator for 20 minutes prior to serving.*

Nutrition per serving
CALORIES: 475 **FAT:** 39g **NET CARBS:** 2g **PROTEIN:** 31g

SNACKS
AND
APPETIZERS

SERVES: 4
SERVING SIZE: 3 WINGS

PREP: 2 HOURS 4 MINUTES
PRESSURE: 7 MINUTES
TOTAL: 2 HOURS 17 MINUTES

SETTING: PRESSURE COOK
RELEASE: NATURAL/QUICK

12 bone-in, skin-on chicken wings
2 tbsp chopped scallions

FOR THE MARINADE
⅓ cup avocado oil
½ tbsp apple cider vinegar
1½ tsp erythritol granular sweetener
1 tsp fine grind sea salt
1 tsp ground allspice
1 tsp onion powder
½ tsp garlic powder
½ tsp ground black pepper
½ tsp ground nutmeg
½ tsp ground ginger
¼ tsp ground cayenne pepper
¼ tsp ground cinnamon
¼ tsp dried thyme leaves

JERK-STYLE CHICKEN WINGS

Rich, fragrant Jamaican spices make these wings mildly spicy, but they're still lightly sweet with just a hint of cinnamon. These are a delicious appetizer that is very low in carbs but big on flavor!

1 Line a large baking sheet with aluminum foil. Set aside.

2 Make the marinade by combining the avocado oil, vinegar, sweetener, sea salt, allspice, onion powder, garlic powder, black pepper, nutmeg, ginger, cayenne pepper, cinnamon, and thyme in a large bowl. Whisk until well combined.

3 Add the chicken wings to the marinade and toss to coat. Cover the bowl with plastic wrap and place in the refrigerator to marinate for 2 hours.

4 Place the steam rack in the inner pot and add 1 cup cold water to the bottom of the pot.

5 Once the marinating time is complete, remove the chicken wings from the refrigerator and stack them on the steam rack.

6 Cover, lock the lid, and flip the steam release handle to the sealing position. Select **Pressure Cook (High)** and set the cook time for **7 minutes.**

7 While the chicken is cooking, preheat the oven broiler to 550°F (288°C).

8 When the cook time for the chicken is complete, allow the pressure to release naturally for 10 minutes and then quick release the remaining pressure.

9 Open the lid and use tongs to transfer the chicken wings to the prepared baking sheet. Place the wings under the broiler to brown for 6 minutes, flipping them halfway through the cooking time.

10 Remove the wings from the oven and transfer them to a serving plate. Sprinkle the scallions over top. Serve hot.

tip *For spicier wings, add an extra ¼ tsp cayenne pepper to the marinade.*

Nutrition per serving
CALORIES: 340 **FAT:** 30g **NET CARBS:** 2g **PROTEIN:** 14g

SAUSAGE-STUFFED MUSHROOMS

These savory sausage-stuffed mushroom caps are rich and cheesy. They're low in carbs, gluten-free, and perfect as bite-sized keto appetizers or as a satisfying snack.

SERVES: 4
SERVING SIZE: 3 MUSHROOMS

PREP: 5 MINUTES
PRESSURE: 20 MINUTES
TOTAL: 40 MINUTES

SETTINGS: SAUTÉ/PRESSURE COOK
RELEASE: QUICK

1 Spray a 6.5-inch (16.5cm) ovenproof soufflé dish with nonstick coconut oil spray. Set aside.

2 Select **Sauté (Normal).** Once the pot is hot, crumble the sausage into the pot. Sauté for 6 minutes or until the sausage is browned and cooked through. Add the garlic, stir, and continue sautéing until the garlic is soft and fragrant.

3 Add the cream cheese, 1 tbsp Parmesan, garlic powder, onion powder, parsley, and black pepper. Stir until the ingredients are combined and the cream cheese is melted, and then press **Cancel** to turn off the pot. Transfer the sausage mixture to a large bowl. Set aside.

4 Remove the inner pot from the base, rinse and wipe dry with a paper towel, and then return the pot to the base. Place the steam rack in the inner pot and add 1 cup water to the bottom of the pot.

5 Arrange the mushroom caps in the prepared soufflé dish with the stem sides facing up. Spoon the sausage mixture into the mushroom caps. Place the soufflé dish on the steam rack.

6 Cover, lock the lid, and flip the steam release handle to the sealing position. Select **Pressure Cook (High)** and set the cook time for **20 minutes.**

7 While the mushrooms are cooking, preheat the oven broiler to 450°F (232°C).

8 When the cook time for the mushrooms is complete, quick release the pressure.

9 Open the lid and carefully remove the soufflé dish from the pot. Sprinkle the almond flour and remaining Parmesan over top of the mushroom caps. Place the dish in the oven and broil for 3 minutes or until the toppings begin to brown.

10 Remove the dish from oven. Using tongs, transfer the mushroom caps to a serving platter. Serve hot.

¼lb (115g) no-sugar-added ground pork sausage

1 garlic clove, minced

3oz (85g) block-style cream cheese, softened and cubed

2 tbsp shredded Parmesan cheese, divided

½ tsp garlic powder

½ tsp onion powder

½ tsp dried parsley

¼ tsp ground black pepper

12 large white button mushrooms, stems removed

1 tbsp almond flour

tip *You can substitute cremini mushrooms for the white button mushrooms.*

Nutrition per serving
CALORIES: 204 **FAT:** 17g **NET CARBS:** 3g **PROTEIN:** 9g

SERVES: 4
SERVING SIZE: 3 WINGS

PREP: 5 MINUTES
PRESSURE: 7 MINUTES
TOTAL: 22 MINUTES

SETTING: PRESSURE COOK
RELEASE: QUICK

1 tsp smoked paprika

½ tsp garlic powder

1 tsp fine grind sea salt

½ tsp ground black pepper

¼ tsp celery seed

⅛ tsp ground cayenne pepper

1½ tbsp olive oil

12 bone-in, skin-on chicken wings

¼ cup hot pepper sauce

4 tbsp unsalted butter

2 tbsp chopped cilantro (optional)

tip *For some extra heat, add an additional ⅛ tsp to ¼ tsp of ground cayenne pepper.*

BUFFALO CHICKEN WINGS

These spicy and saucy keto buffalo wings are low in carbs, gluten-free, and just as rich and buttery as the wings from your favorite wing restaurant but without the deep frying!

1 In a small bowl, combine the smoked paprika, garlic powder, sea salt, black pepper, celery seed, cayenne pepper, and olive oil. Stir until well combined. Set aside.

2 In a large bowl, combine the chicken wings and spice mixture. Using tongs, toss the chicken to coat in the spice mixture.

3 Place the steam rack in the inner pot and add ⅔ cup cold water to the bottom of the pot. Stack the seasoned wings on the rack.

4 Cover, lock the lid, and flip the steam release handle to the sealing position. Select **Pressure Cook (High)** and set the cook time for **7 minutes.**

5 While the chicken is cooking, preheat the oven broiler to 550°F (288°C) and line a large baking sheet with aluminum foil. Spray the foil with nonstick coconut oil spray. Set aside.

6 Combine the hot pepper sauce and butter in a small saucepan and place over medium heat. Cook, stirring continuously, until the butter has melted and the ingredients are combined. Cover, reduce the heat to low, and simmer for 3 minutes and then remove from the pan from the heat. Set aside.

7 When the cook time for the chicken is complete, quick release the pressure. Open the lid and use tongs to transfer wings to a large bowl. Pour half the buffalo sauce over the wings and use tongs to coat the wings in the buffalo sauce.

8 Arrange the wings on the foil-lined baking sheet. Place the baking sheet on a rack positioned just above the center of the oven, vent the oven door, and broil for 6 minutes, flipping the wings halfway through the cooking time.

9 Stir the remaining buffalo sauce. Using a pastry brush, brush the sauce over the wings and then transfer the wings to a serving platter. Sprinkle the cilantro over top (if using). Serve warm.

Nutrition per serving
CALORIES: 326   **FAT:** 27g   **NET CARBS:** 1g   **PROTEIN:** 16g

SERVES: 5
SERVING SIZE: 2 POPPERS

PREP: 5 MINUTES
PRESSURE: 4 MINUTES
TOTAL: 28 MINUTES

SETTINGS: SAUTÉ/PRESSURE COOK
RELEASE: QUICK

10 slices uncooked bacon

5 medium jalapeño peppers, halved lengthwise, stems and seeds removed

4oz (110g) block-style cream cheese, softened and cubed

¼ cup shredded mozzarella cheese

¼ tsp fine grind sea salt

⅛ tsp ground black pepper

¼ tsp dried parsley

¼ tsp onion powder

¼ tsp ground cumin

tip *For a higher level of heat, substitute serrano peppers for the jalapeño peppers.*

JALAPEÑO BACON POPPERS

This keto classic features warm jalapeño peppers filled with a creamy spiced cheese filling and wrapped in smoky bacon. These are low in carbs, gluten-free, and provide a perfectly balanced bite of flavors.

1 Line a large baking sheet with aluminum foil. Set aside.

2 Select **Sauté (Normal)**. Once the pot is hot, add half the bacon and sauté for 4 minutes per side or until the bacon is partially cooked on both sides. Transfer the bacon slices to a plate lined with a paper towel to drain. Repeat with the remaining slices. Set aside.

3 Add the jalapeño pepper halves to the pot. Sauté in the bacon grease for 4 minutes per side or until the skin begins to blister. Transfer the jalapeños to a plate lined with a paper towel to drain. Press **Cancel** to turn off heat and remove the inner pot from the base to cool.

4 Once the inner pot is cool enough to handle, rinse and wipe dry with a paper towel, and then return the pot to the base. Place the steam rack in the inner pot and add 1 cup water to the bottom of the pot.

5 In a large bowl, combine the cream cheese, mozzarella, sea salt, black pepper, parsley, onion powder, and cumin. Mix until well combined.

6 Spoon equal amounts of the cream cheese mixture into each jalapeño shell and then wrap a partially cooked slice of bacon around each shell. Place the stuffed peppers skin-side-down on the steam rack.

7 Cover, lock the lid, and flip the steam release handle to the sealing position. Select **Pressure Cook (Low)** and set the cook time for **4 minutes.**

8 While the jalapeños are cooking, preheat the oven broiler to 550°F (288°C).

9 When the cook time for the jalapeños is complete, quick release the pressure.

10 Using tongs, transfer the poppers to the lined baking sheet and place under the broiler for 3 minutes or until the bacon becomes crisp.

11 Remove the poppers from the oven and transfer to a serving platter. Serve warm.

Nutrition per serving
CALORIES: 181 **FAT:** 16g **NET CARBS:** 3g **PROTEIN:** 8g

RATATOUILLE DIP

This warm and colorful vegetable dip is served with crunchy fresh cucumber chips. This keto take on a classic French dish is low in carbs and gluten-free, and it makes a satisfying snack.

SERVES: 4
SERVING SIZE: ½ CUP WITH 3 CUCUMBER SLICES

PREP: 8 MINUTES
PRESSURE: 10 MINUTES
TOTAL: 26 MINUTES

SETTINGS: SAUTÉ/PRESSURE COOK
RELEASE: QUICK

1 Spray a 6-inch (15.25cm) soufflé dish with nonstick olive oil cooking spray. Set aside.

2 Add the eggplant to a medium bowl. Sprinkle with the sea salt and toss to coat. Set aside.

3 Select **Sauté (Normal).** Add 2 tbsp olive oil to the inner pot. Once the oil is hot, add the garlic, zucchini, and yellow squash. Sauté for 3 minutes or until the squash becomes soft.

4 Add the bell peppers and basil leaves to the pot and sauté for 4 additional minutes. Transfer the squash mixture to the prepared soufflé dish. Set aside.

5 Remove the eggplant from the bowl and transfer to a plate lined with paper towels to drain for 3 minutes.

6 Add the remaining olive oil to the pot. Add the eggplant and sauté for 4 minutes or until the eggplant has softened. Press **Cancel** to turn off the pot.

7 Transfer the eggplant to the soufflé dish. Add the tomato sauce and red pepper flakes and gently stir. Arrange the tomato slices on top. Set aside.

8 Carefully remove the inner pot from the base, rinse and wipe dry with a paper towel, and then return the pot to the base. Place the steam rack in the inner pot and add 1 cup water to the pot. Place the soufflé dish on the steamer rack.

9 Cover, lock the lid, and flip the steam release handle to the sealing position. Select **Pressure Cook (High)** and set the cook time for **10 minutes.** When the cook time is complete, quick release the pressure.

10 Open the lid and carefully remove the soufflé dish from the pot. Sprinkle the parsley over top and serve with the cucumber slices on the side for dipping. Serve warm.

1 cup diced eggplant

½ tbsp fine grind sea salt

4 tbsp extra virgin olive oil, divided

3 garlic cloves, minced

⅔ cup diced zucchini

½ cup diced yellow squash

2 mini bell peppers, cored, seeded, and thinly sliced

4 fresh basil leaves

⅓ cup no-sugar-added tomato sauce

½ tsp crushed red pepper flakes

1 large tomato, cut into 4 thick slices

2 tbsp chopped flat-leaf parsley

1 English cucumber, cut into 12 thick slices (to serve)

tip *If you don't have yellow squash, you can substitute an additional ½ cup diced zucchini.*

Nutrition per serving
CALORIES: 167   **FAT:** 15g   **NET CARBS:** 6g   **PROTEIN:** 2g

TACO-STUFFED MINI BELL PEPPERS

You can still eat Mexican food on a keto diet! This South-of-the-border-style snack tastes like a taco but without the high-carb shell. These low-carb mini appetizers are the perfect finger food!

 SERVES: 5
SERVING SIZE: 2 PEPPERS

 PREP: 5 MINUTES
PRESSURE: 2 MINUTES
TOTAL: 50 MINUTES

SETTINGS: SAUTÉ/PRESSURE COOK
RELEASE: QUICK

1 Select **Sauté** and add the olive oil to the pot. Once the oil is hot, add the peppers and sauté for 3 minutes or until the sides just begin to blister. Transfer the peppers to a large plate. Set aside.

2 Add the ground beef to the inner pot. Sauté for 4 minutes or until the meat is browned, using a wooden spoon to stir and break up the meat.

3 Add the tomato sauce, chili powder, cumin, garlic powder, onion powder, paprika, and sea salt to the pot. Stir. Heat the mixture until it begins to bubble, stirring continuously, and then transfer the mixture to a medium bowl. Press **Cancel** to turn off the pot.

4 Spoon the ground beef mixture into the bell pepper halves.

5 Place the steam rack in the pot and add 1 cup water to the bottom of the pot. Place a steamer basket with legs on top of the rack and place the stuffed peppers skin-side-down in the steamer basket.

6 Cover, lock the lid, and flip the steam release handle to the sealing position. Select **Pressure Cook (Low)** and set the cook time for **2 minutes.** When the cook time is complete, quick release the pressure.

7 Open the lid and sprinkle the cheddar over top of the peppers. Replace the lid to warm and melt the cheese for 2 minutes.

8 Open the lid and transfer the peppers to a serving platter. Top each pepper with black olives and a small dollop of sour cream. Sprinkle the cilantro over top (if using). Serve warm.

½ tbsp olive oil

5 mini bell peppers, cut in half lengthwise, and seeds removed

⅓lb (151g) ground beef

⅓ cup no-sugar-added tomato sauce

½ tsp chili powder

¼ tsp ground cumin

¼ tsp garlic powder

⅛ tsp onion powder

⅛ tsp paprika

¼ tsp fine grind sea salt

⅓ cup shredded cheddar cheese

1 tbsp sliced black olives

2 tbsp full-fat sour cream

1 tbsp chopped fresh cilantro (optional)

tip *To make this recipe dairy-free, substitute ⅓ cup shredded almond cheese for the cheddar cheese and omit the sour cream.*

Nutrition per serving
CALORIES: 135 **FAT:** 9g **NET CARBS:** 4g **PROTEIN:** 9g

SERVES: 8
SERVING SIZE: 4½ TBSP DIP WITH 3 CELERY STICKS

PREP: 5 MINUTES
PRESSURE: 12 MINUTES
TOTAL: 17 MINUTES

SETTING: PRESSURE COOK
RELEASE: QUICK

8oz (225g) block-style cream cheese, softened and cubed

10oz (285g) box frozen spinach, thawed and drained

1 cup canned artichoke hearts, drained and chopped

½ cup shredded Parmesan cheese

½ cup shredded mozzarella cheese

½ cup shredded Monterey Jack cheese

⅓ cup chicken broth

½ cup full-fat sour cream

¼ cup mayonnaise

3 garlic cloves, minced

1 tsp onion powder

¼ tsp fine grind sea salt

¼ tsp ground black pepper

8 stalks celery, cut into thirds (to serve)

ARTICHOKE SPINACH VEGGIE DIP

Packed with healthy spinach and artichokes, this creamy, easy-to-prepare keto dip is warm and cheesy, and the perfect flavor-filled dip for crunchy vegetables.

1 In a 6 x 3-inch (15.25 x 7.5cm) 1-quart (1l) soufflé dish, combine the cream cheese, spinach, artichoke hearts, Parmesan, mozzarella, Monterey Jack, chicken broth, sour cream, mayonnaise, garlic, onion powder, sea salt, and black pepper. Gently stir until the ingredients are just combined.

2 Tightly cover the top of the soufflé dish with a sheet of aluminum foil.

3 Add 1 cup water to the bottom of the inner pot. Place the covered dish on the steam rack and carefully lower the rack into the pot.

4 Cover, lock the lid, and flip the steam release handle to the sealing position. Select **Pressure Cook (High)** and set the cook time for **12 minutes.** When the cook time is complete, quick release the pressure.

5 Open the lid, grasp the rack handles, and carefully lift the rack and dish out of the pot. Remove the aluminum foil and use a large fork to stir the dip vigorously until the ingredients are well combined.

6 Transfer the dish to a serving platter. Serve promptly with the celery sticks on the side for dipping.

tip *This dip also doubles as a wonderful low-carb sauce that can be served over chicken.*

Nutrition per serving
CALORIES: 362 **FAT:** 25g **NET CARBS:** 7g **PROTEIN:** 17g

CHILE QUESO DIP
with Crudités

Smooth and creamy, this rich, cheesy dip has warm Mexican spices and a touch of green chiles for an authentic flavor. Crisp veggies are the perfect accompaniment to this low carb and gluten-free appetizer.

SERVES: 4
SERVING SIZE: 4 TBSP DIP WITH 3 CELERY STICKS

PREP: 3 MINUTES
PRESSURE: 19 MINUTES
TOTAL: 22 MINUTES

SETTING: PRESSURE COOK
RELEASE: NATURAL/QUICK

1   In a 6 x 3-inch (15.25cm x 7.5cm) round baking dish, combine the butter, garlic, chiles, sea salt, chili powder, cheese, sour cream, and heavy cream. Mix well to combine. Tightly cover the dish with a small sheet of aluminum foil.

2   Add 1 cup water to the inner pot. Place the covered dish on the steam rack, grasp the rack handles and carefully lower the rack and dish into the pot.

3   Cover, lock the lid, and flip the steam release handle to the sealing position. Select **Pressure Cook (High)** and set the cook time for **19 minutes.** When the cook time is complete, quick release the pressure.

4   Open the lid, remove and discard the foil, and immediately whisk the dip thoroughly until a smooth, creamy consistency is achieved.

5   Carefully transfer the dish to a serving platter. Place the vegetables on the platter. Serve promptly.

1 tbsp unsalted butter

1 garlic clove, minced

2½ tbsp canned diced green chiles

⅛ tsp fine grind sea salt

¼ tsp chili powder

1½ cups Mexican-blend shredded cheese

6 tbsp sour cream

2 tbsp heavy cream

3 mini bell peppers, halved and seeded (to serve)

4 stalks celery, cut into thirds (to serve)

tip *Depending on your taste preferences, you can use mild or hot green chiles in this recipe.*

This dip also is delicious as a spiced cheese sauce served over steamed vegetables.

Nutrition per serving
CALORIES: 190   **FAT:** 13g   **NET CARBS:** 5g   **PROTEIN:** 5g

SERVES: 4
SERVING SIZE: 4 SPEARS WITH 1 TBSP SAUCE

PREP: 5 MINUTES
PRESSURE: 2 MINUTES
TOTAL: 15 MINUTES

SETTINGS: STEAM/SAUTÉ
RELEASE: QUICK

16 spears asparagus, woody ends removed

8 slices prosciutto, cut in half

1 tbsp olive oil

FOR THE SAUCE

3 tbsp mayonnaise

2 tsp Dijon mustard

1 tsp lemon juice

¼ tsp ground black pepper

PROSCIUTTO-WRAPPED ASPARAGUS
with Creamy Dijon Sauce

Perfectly steamed asparagus is wrapped in smoky, salty prosciutto and seared to lock in the rich flavors. This brilliant low-carb appetizer is a delight for the taste buds when paired with the creamy Dijon sauce.

1 Make the creamy Dijon sauce by combining the mayonnaise, Dijon mustard, lemon juice, and black pepper in a small bowl. Mix well. Cover the bowl with plastic wrap and place in the refrigerator.

2 Place the steam rack in the inner pot and add 1 cup water to the bottom of the pot. Place the asparagus spears on the steam rack.

3 Cover, lock the lid, and flip the steam release handle to the sealing position. Select **Steam (High)** and set the cook time for **2 minutes.** When the cook time is complete, quick release the pressure.

4 Open the lid and carefully grasp the rack handles to remove the steam rack and asparagus from the pot. Set aside.

5 Carefully remove the inner pot from the base, drain and wipe dry with a paper towel, and then return the pot to the base.

6 Wrap each asparagus spear with a half slice of the prosciutto.

7 Select **Sauté (Normal).** Once the pot is hot, add the olive oil and heat for 1 minute. Working in batches, add the wrapped spears to the pot and sauté on all sides for 2 minutes or until just brown, using tongs to rotate the spears. Transfer the sautéed spears to a plate and repeat with the remaining spears.

8 Serve warm with the creamy Dijon sauce served on the side for dipping. (Alternatively, you can drizzle 1 tablespoon of the sauce over top of each serving and serve as a side.)

tip *If you don't have a steamer basket with legs, you can use an ovenproof bowl placed on top of the steam rack.*

Nutrition per serving
CALORIES: 250   **FAT:** 21g   **NET CARBS:** 2g   **PROTEIN:** 16g

SERVES: 5
SERVING SIZE: 3 DRUMETTES

PREP: 10 MINUTES
PRESSURE: 5 MINUTES
TOTAL: 35 MINUTES

SETTING: PRESSURE COOK
RELEASE: NATURAL/QUICK

1 tsp smoked paprika

1 tsp garlic powder

1 tsp fine grind sea salt

¼ tsp ground black pepper

2lbs (1kg) skin-on chicken drumettes

FOR THE SAUCE

⅔ cup no-sugar-added tomato sauce

1 tbsp tomato paste

1½ tbsp erythritol granular sweetener

1 tbsp apple cider vinegar

1½ tsp liquid smoke

½ tbsp Worcestershire sauce

1 tbsp butter, melted

½ tsp molasses

½ tsp garlic powder

½ tsp fine grind sea salt

½ tsp onion powder

tip *To make this recipe dairy-free, substitute 1 tbsp avocado oil for the butter in the sauce.*

BBQ CHICKEN DRUMETTES

You can make saucy, mouth-watering BBQ chicken using just the Instant Pot! This lip-smacking appetizer is drenched in a smoky and tangy barbecue sauce that will have you licking your fingers.

1 Combine all the sauce ingredients in a small saucepan placed over medium heat. Cook, stirring continuously, until the butter is melted. Cover the pan, reduce the heat to low and simmer for 4 minutes, and then remove the pan from the heat. Set aside.

2 In a small bowl, combine the smoked paprika, garlic powder, sea salt, and black pepper. Mix until well combined.

3 Add the drumettes to a large bowl and then add the spice mixture. Using a large spoon, toss the chicken to coat in the spices.

4 Place the steam rack in the inner pot and add ½ cup water to the bottom of the pot. Place the seasoned drumettes on top of the rack.

5 Cover, lock the lid, and flip the steam release handle to the sealing position. Select **Pressure Cook (High)** and set the cook time for **5 minutes.**

6 While chicken is cooking, line a large baking sheet with aluminum foil and spray with nonstick coconut oil spray. Preheat the oven broiler to 550°F (288°C).

7 When the cook time for the chicken is complete, allow the pressure to release naturally for 10 minutes and then quick release the remaining pressure.

8 Open the lid and transfer the drumettes to a large bowl. Pour half the barbeque sauce over the chicken. Using a large spoon, toss the drumettes to coat in sauce.

9 Transfer the drumettes to the foil-lined baking sheet and place the baking sheet on a rack positioned just above the center of the oven. Leaving the oven door slightly open to vent, broil the drumettes for 10 minutes, flipping the them halfway through the cook time.

10 Remove the drumettes from oven and place them in the bowl with the sauce. Pour the remaining barbecue sauce over top and toss again to coat. Transfer to a serving platter. Serve warm.

Nutrition per serving
CALORIES: 391   **FAT:** 27g   **NET CARBS:** 3g   **PROTEIN:** 30g

DEVILED EGGS
with Bacon and Chives

These rich and creamy eggs are filled with fragrant spices and topped with a sprinkle of smoky bacon. They're a delight for your taste buds, low carb, gluten-free, and perfect for a satisfying snack or appetizer.

SERVES: 6
SERVING SIZE: 2 EGGS

PREP: 8 MINUTES
PRESSURE: 5 MINUTES
TOTAL: 1 HOUR

SETTING: PRESSURE COOK
RELEASE: NATURAL/QUICK

6 large eggs
⅓ cup mayonnaise
1 tsp Dijon mustard
½ tsp white vinegar
½ tsp hot pepper sauce
⅛ tsp ground black pepper
⅛ tsp fine grind sea salt
¼ tsp paprika
2 slices cooked bacon, crumbled
1 tsp chives, chopped

1 Create an ice water bath by filling a large bowl halfway with cold water and ice. Set aside.

2 Place the steam rack in the inner pot and add 1 cup cold water to the bottom of the pot. Place the eggs on the steam rack.

3 Cover, lock the lid, and flip the steam release handle to the sealing position. Select **Pressure Cook (High)** and set the cook time for **5 minutes.**

4 When the cook time is complete, allow the pressure to release naturally for 5 minutes and then quick release the remaining pressure.

5 Open the lid and use a slotted spoon to carefully transfer the eggs to the ice water bath. Let the eggs cool in the bath for 5 minutes.

6 Once the eggs are cool enough to handle, use a slotted spoon to remove the eggs from the ice bath. Peel the eggs and cut each in half lengthwise.

7 Using a small spoon, carefully scoop the yolks from the whites and place the yolks in a medium bowl. Place the egg white halves on a platter and set aside.

8 Using a fork, mash the egg yolks. Add the mayonnaise, Dijon mustard, vinegar, hot pepper sauce, black pepper, and sea salt. Mix until no lumps remain and a creamy texture is achieved.

9 Spoon the yolk mixture into a pastry bag with a large tip and pipe 1 tablespoon of the mixture into each egg white half.

10 Sprinkle the bacon crumbles and paprika over top of each egg and garnish with the chives. Transfer to a resealable container and refrigerate for a minimum of 30 minutes. Serve chilled.

tip *If you don't have a pastry bag, you can create one by filling a large plastic zipper-lock bag as you would a pastry bag and then cutting one corner from the bag.*

Nutrition per serving
CALORIES: 163   **FAT:** 14g   **NET CARBS:** 1g   **PROTEIN:** 7g

DESSERTS

CRUSTLESS KEY LIME PIE

This creamy key lime pie is rich and indulgent, and topped with a fluffy whipped topping. It has all the sweet and tangy flavors of key lime pie but without all the carbs from a crust!

SERVES: 8
SERVING SIZE: 1 SLICE

PREP: 8 MINUTES
PRESSURE: 44 MINUTES
TOTAL: 8 HOURS 55 MINUTES

SETTING: PRESSURE COOK
RELEASE: NATURAL

1 Line a 6x3-inch (15.25x7.5cm) springform pan with trimmed parchment paper. Spray the inside of the pan and the parchment paper with nonstick coconut oil spray. Set aside.

2 In a large mixing bowl, combine the cream cheese, sweetener, vanilla extract, and coconut flour. Using a hand mixer or stand mixer, beat the ingredients on medium until combined. Continue to beat until thoroughly blended, scraping the sides of the bowl with a spatula.

3 Add the eggs to the bowl, one at a time, and beat until just combined. Add the egg yolk and beat until just combined. Add the key lime juice and continue to beat until the ingredients are well combined.

4 Pour the mixture into the prepared pan. Cover the top of the pan with a paper towel and then tightly cover the pan with aluminum foil.

5 Place the steam rack in the inner pot and add 1½ cups water to the bottom of the pot. Place the springform pan on top of the rack.

6 Cover, lock the lid, and flip the steam release handle to the sealing position. Select **Pressure Cook (High)** and set the cook time for **44 minutes.** When the cook time is complete, allow the pressure to release naturally (about 20 minutes).

7 Open the lid, carefully grasp the steam rack handles, and lift the rack and pan out of the pot. Remove the aluminum foil and discard the paper towel. (Use a paper towel to gently blot away any moisture that has accumulated on top of the pie.) Let the pie cool to room temperature (about 30 minutes) and then re-cover with the foil and place in the refrigerator to set for a minimum of 8 hours.

8 Make the topping by combining the whipping cream and sweetener in a large bowl. Using an immersion blender or hand mixer, whip until the mixture becomes stiff. Cover and refrigerate.

9 After the chilling time for the pie is complete, run a butter knife around the inside of the pan to loosen the pie from the sides of the pan, and then carefully remove the outer ring of the pan.

10 Transfer the pie to a serving platter and slice into 8 equal-sized wedges. Top each serving with 2 tbsp of the whipped topping. Serve chilled.

16oz (450g) block-style cream cheese, softened

⅔ cup erythritol and oligosaccharide blend granular sweetener

1½ tsp vanilla extract

1½ tsp coconut flour

2 large eggs

1 egg yolk

4 tbsp key lime juice (fresh or concentrate)

FOR THE WHIPPED TOPPING

½ cup heavy whipping cream

1½ tbsp erythritol and oligosaccharide blend granular sweetener

tip *If you don't have key lime juice, you can substitute an equal amount of regular lime juice.*

Nutrition per serving
CALORIES: 289   **FAT:** 27g   **NET CARBS:** 4g   **PROTEIN:** 6g

SERVES: 4
SERVING SIZE: 5OZ (140G)

PREP: 5 MINUTES
COOK: 10 HOURS 25 MINUTES
TOTAL: 17 HOURS

SETTINGS: YOGURT/YOGURT
RELEASE: NONE

2 cups unsweetened full-fat coconut cream

½ cup heavy cream

4 probiotic capsules

½ tbsp unflavored gelatin powder

½ tsp vanilla extract

⅛ tsp ground vanilla bean

¼ tsp stevia extract

½ cup fresh blueberries

__tip__ To make this recipe dairy-free, substitute coconut cream for the heavy cream.

Probiotic capsules can be found at health food stores, or in drug stores in the supplement and vitamin section.

VANILLA YOGURT
with Fresh Blueberries

This creamy, tangy homemade yogurt is keto-friendly and features fresh blueberries with hints of vanilla. Making yogurt in the Instant Pot means it's free of unhealthy additives and full of gut-friendly probiotics.

1 Make an ice water bath by filling a large bowl halfway with ice and cold water. Set aside.

2 Combine the coconut cream and heavy cream in the inner pot.

3 Cover and lock lid, but leave the steam release handle in the venting position. Select **Yogurt (More)** until the **Boil** setting appears on the display.

4 Once the boil cycle is complete (about 25 minutes), open the lid and carefully transfer the inner pot to the ice water bath. Allow the mixture to cool in the ice water bath until the mixture reaches 110°F (43°C). (Use a candy thermometer to check the temperature.)

5 Once the mixture reaches the target temperature, break open the probiotic capsules, add the capsule contents to the mixture, and then discard the empty capsules. Whisk the ingredients until thoroughly combined.

6 Remove the inner pot from the ice water bath, wipe the exterior of the pot dry with a paper towel, and then return the pot to the base. Replace the lid, select **Yogurt,** and set the cook time for **10 hours.**

7 When the cook time is complete, open the lid and add the gelatin, a small amount at a time, while whisking the mixture continuously. Continue whisking until the ingredients are thoroughly combined.

8 Add the vanilla extract, ground vanilla bean, and stevia extract. Stir.

9 Transfer the yogurt to four 5oz (150ml) resealable containers. Seal and place in the refrigerator to thicken for a minimum of 8 hours.

10 Once the chilling time is complete, remove the jars from the refridgerator, remove the lids, and top each serving with equal amounts of the blueberries. Serve chilled.

Nutrition per serving
CALORIES: 313   **FAT:** 30g   **NET CARBS:** 5g   **PROTEIN:** 2g

CHOCOLATE COCONUT MOUSSE

Creamy, rich, and delicious, this decadent mousse is accented with subtle accents of coconut and vanilla. You'll be amazed that this utterly divine dessert is both low carb and sugar-free.

SERVES: 5
SERVING SIZE: 1 RAMEKIN

PREP: 10 MINUTES
PRESSURE: 6 MINUTES
TOTAL: 5 HOURS 20 MINUTES

SETTING: PRESSURE COOK
RELEASE: QUICK

4 egg yolks
¼ cup water
½ cup erythritol granular sweetener
¼ cup cocoa powder
½ cup unsweetened coconut milk
¾ cup heavy cream
½ tsp vanilla extract
⅛ tsp fine grind sea salt
1 tbsp unsweetened, finely shredded coconut

1 Place the steam rack in the inner pot and add 1½ cups water to the bottom of the pot.

2 Add the egg yolks to a medium bowl. Whisk and set aside.

3 In a small saucepan placed over medium heat, combine the water, sweetener, and cocoa powder. Whisk until the ingredients are combined and the sweetener has dissolved.

4 Add the coconut milk and heavy cream to the pan. Whisk until combined and then remove the pan from the heat. Add the vanilla and sea salt, stir, and let the mixture cool for 3 minutes.

5 Whisk 2 tablespoons of the warm chocolate mixture into the egg yolks. Slowly add the remaining mixture while continuously whisking until the ingredients are thoroughly combined.

6 Equally divide the mixture between five 3 x 2-inch (7.5 x 5cm) ramekins. Place the ramekins on top of the steam rack.

7 Cover, lock the lid, and flip the steam release handle to the sealing position. Select **Pressure Cook (High)** and set the cook time for **6 minutes.** Once the cook time is complete, quick release the pressure.

8 Open the lid and carefully transfer the ramekins to a heat-safe surface. Let cool to room temperature.

9 Tightly cover the cooled ramekins with plastic wrap and place in the refrigerator to chill for a minimum of 5 hours.

10 Remove the chilled ramekins from the fridge, remove and discard the plastic wrap, and sprinkle ½ teaspoon shredded coconut over top of each serving. Serve chilled.

tip *To make this recipe dairy-free, substitute coconut milk for the heavy cream.*

Nutrition per serving
CALORIES: 244 **FAT:** 25g **NET CARBS:** 3g **PROTEIN:** 4g

SERVES: 2
SERVING SIZE: 1 CAKE

PREP: 8 MINUTES
PRESSURE: 25 MINUTES
TOTAL: 35 MINUTES

SETTING: PRESSURE COOK
RELEASE: QUICK

½ cup peeled and diced jicama

4 tbsp erythritol and oligosaccharide blend granular sweetener, divided

½ tbsp finely chopped walnuts (optional)

¾ tsp ground cinnamon, divided

⅔ cup almond flour

1 tsp baking powder

¼ tsp ground nutmeg

¼ tsp allspice

⅛ tsp fine grind sea salt

2 large eggs

1½ tbsp heavy cream

1 tsp vanilla extract

FOR THE SAUCE

2 tbsp butter

2 tbsp heavy cream

1 tbsp erythritol and oligosaccharide blend granular sweetener

⅛ tsp vanilla extract

tip *Jicama can be found in most grocery store produce sections, or in natural food stores.*

CARAMEL JICAMA MINI CAKES

Warm apple pie spices and a gooey, buttery caramel sauce add a decadent finish to this sweet treat, which features jicama to mimic the taste and texture of an apple cake.

1 Lightly coat two 3.5 x 2.5-inch (9 x 5cm) ramekins with nonstick coconut oil spray.

2 In a medium bowl, combine the jicama, 1 tbsp sweetener, walnuts (if using), and ¼ tsp cinnamon. With a spoon, gently fold the jicama and walnuts to coat in the sweetener and cinnamon. Set aside.

3 In a large bowl, combine the almond flour, remaining sweetener, baking powder, remaining cinnamon, nutmeg, allspice, and sea salt. Mix to combine.

4 Add the eggs, heavy cream, and vanilla extract to the bowl, and whisk until no lumps remain. Fold the jicama mixture into the batter.

5 Spoon equal amounts of the batter into the ramekins and use a spoon to smooth. Tightly cover each ramekin with aluminum foil.

6 Add 2 cups water to the bottom of the inner pot. Place the ramekins on the steam rack, grasp the steam rack handles, and carefully lower the rack and ramekins into the pot.

7 Cover, lock the lid, and flip the steam release handle to the sealing position. Select **Pressure Cook (High)** and set the cook time for **25 minutes.**

8 When the cook time is complete, quick release the pressure. Open the lid and carefully transfer the ramekins to a cooling rack.

9 Make the caramel sauce by melting the butter in a small saucepan placed over medium heat. Add the heavy cream and sweetener and stir until the sauce is bubbling and begins to thicken.

10 Remove the pan from the heat and stir in the vanilla extract. Allow the sauce to cool and thicken in the pan for 2 minutes.

11 Drizzle 2 tablespoons of the caramel sauce over top of each cake. Serve warm.

Nutrition per serving
CALORIES: 435   **FAT:** 40g   **NET CARBS:** 6g   **PROTEIN:** 15g

SERVES: 4
SERVING SIZE: ⅓ CUP
WITH 4 RASPBERRIESS

PREP: 5 MINUTES
PRESSURE: 12 MINUTES
TOTAL: 4 HOURS 57 MINUTES

SETTING: PRESSURE COOK
RELEASE: NATURAL

⅓ cup unsweetened vanilla almond milk

3½ tbsp erythritol granular sweetener

⅔ cup heavy cream

1 tsp vanilla extract

2 large egg yolks

16 fresh raspberries

tip *To make this recipe dairy-free, substitute ⅔ cup full-fat coconut milk for the heavy cream.*

VANILLA PUDDING
with Fresh Raspberries

This thick and creamy pudding has a distinctive vanilla flavor and is topped with fresh raspberries. This keto treat is extremely low in carbs and delightfully sweet.

1 Combine the almond milk and sweetener in a small saucepan placed over medium heat. Whisk until the sweetener is dissolved. Remove from the heat and let cool for 5 minutes.

2 Add the heavy cream and vanilla to the pan and whisk until well combined. Set aside.

3 In a medium bowl, whisk the egg yolks until smooth. Set aside.

4 Place the steam rack in the inner pot and add 2 cups cold water to the bottom of the pot.

5 Slowly add the cream mixture to the egg yolks. Whisk continuously until combined.

6 Evenly divide the mixture across four 3-ounce (85g) ramekins. Tightly cover each ramekin with a small sheet of aluminum foil.

7 Place the covered ramekins on the steam rack. (You can stack one ramekin on top of the other three if they won't all fit on the rack.)

8 Cover, lock the lid, and flip the steam release handle to the sealing position. Select **Pressure Cook (High)** and set the cook time for **12 minutes.** When the cook time is complete, allow the pressure to release naturally (about 20 minutes).

9 Open the lid and use tongs to carefully transfer the ramekins to a cooling rack. Remove the foil and let the ramekins cool to room temperature (about 20 minutes).

10 Tightly cover the cooled ramekins with plastic wrap and place in the refrigerator to set for 4 hours. Once set, remove the ramekins from the refrigerator, discard the plastic wrap, and top each ramekin with four raspberries. Serve chilled.

Nutrition per serving
CALORIES: 175   **FAT:** 17g   **NET CARBS:** 2g   **PROTEIN:** 2g

LEMON BLUEBERRY POKE CAKE

This sweet and tart lemon cake is full of fresh blueberries and topped with a refreshing glaze that oozes into the cake by way of holes poked in the cake. It's satisfyingly sweet, low carb, and gluten-free!

SERVES: 8
SERVING SIZE: 1 PIECE

PREP: 8 MINUTES
PRESSURE: 39 MINUTES
TOTAL: 1 HOUR 15 MINUTES

SETTING: PRESSURE COOK
RELEASE: NATURAL/QUICK

1 Add 1½ cups water to the inner pot. Generously spray a 6 x 3-inch (15.25 x 7.5cm) aluminum cake pan with coconut oil spray. Set aside.

2 In a large bowl, combine the coconut flour, sweetener, baking powder, baking soda, and sea salt. Mix thoroughly. Set aside.

3 In a separate large bowl, combine the eggs, almond milk, melted coconut oil, lemon juice, lemon extract, and lemon zest. Mix thoroughly.

4 Make the batter by adding the wet ingredients to the dry ingredients and stirring until the ingredients are well combined and no lumps remain. Add the blueberries and gently fold into the batter.

5 Spoon the batter into the prepared pan and use a knife to spread batter evenly in the pan. Tightly cover the pan with aluminum foil, place the pan on the steam rack, and carefully lower the rack into the pot.

6 Cover, lock the lid, and flip the steam release handle to the sealing position. Select **Pressure Cook (High)** and set the cook time for **39 minutes.** When the cook time is complete, allow the pressure to release naturally for 10 minutes and then quick release the remaining pressure.

7 Open the lid and carefully grasp the steam rack handles to lift the rack and pan out of the pot. Remove the foil from pan and use a paper towel to gently blot away any moisture that's formed on the surface of the cake. Let the cake cool in the pan for 6 minutes.

8 While the cake cools, make the glaze by melting the butter in a small saucepan placed over medium heat. Add the heavy cream, sweetener, and lemon juice. Stirring continuously, cook until the sweetener dissolves and the glaze begins to thicken, and then remove the pan from the heat. Add the lemon extract and lemon zest. Stir.

9 Using a wooden spoon or metal skewer, poke several evenly spaced holes across the top of the cake. Pour the glaze over top of the cake. Tightly cover the cake with plastic wrap and place in the refrigerator for a minimum of 15 minutes to allow the glaze to become solid.

10 Remove the cake from the refrigerator and slice into 8-equal sized pieces. Serve cool.

½ cup coconut flour, sifted

½ cup erythritol and oligosaccharide blend granular sweetener

1 tsp baking powder

¼ tsp baking soda

⅛ tsp fine grind sea salt

3 large eggs

½ cup unsweetened almond milk

2 tbsp coconut oil, melted

1½ tbsp lemon juice

1 tsp lemon extract

2 tsp freshly grated lemon zest

⅓ cup fresh blueberries

FOR THE GLAZE

2 tbsp butter

2 tbsp heavy cream

2½ tbsp erythritol and oligosaccharide blend confectioners' powdered sweetener

2 tsp lemon juice

½ tsp lemon extract

½ tsp freshly grated lemon zest

tip *Don't use a springform pan for this recipe—the ingredients will leak from the bottom of the pan.*

Nutrition per serving
CALORIES: 155 **FAT:** 11g **NET CARBS:** 4g **PROTEIN:** 4g

MIXED BERRY CINNAMON CRISP
with Whipped Cream

This lovely dessert features warm, sweet berries, a buttery cinnamon crumble, and a dollop of sugar-free whipped cream on top. You'll be making this delicious treat over and over again!

1 Spray a round 7 x 3-inch (17.5 x 7.5cm) ceramic baking dish with nonstick coconut oil spray. Place the steam rack in the inner pot and add 1 cup water to the bottom of the pot.

2 In a large bowl, combine the berries, ⅓ cup sweetener, and xanthan gum. Using a spoon, gently toss the berries to coat with the ingredients and then transfer the mixture to the prepared baking dish. Set aside.

3 In a separate large bowl, combine the almond flour, coconut, remaining sweetener, cinnamon, and melted butter. Mix until a crumbly texture is formed.

4 Spoon the crumble mixture over top of the berries. Place a sheet of foil underneath the dish and fold the edges up around the sides of the dish. Cover the dish with a paper towel and then cover the paper towel with an additional sheet of foil. Fold the edges of the foil down to tightly wrap the entire dish in the foil. Place the dish on the steam rack.

5 Cover, lock the lid, and flip the steam release handle to the sealing position. Select **Pressure Cook (High)** and set the cook time for **15 minutes.** When the cook time is complete, quick release the pressure.

6 While the crisp is cooking, preheat the oven broiler to 550°F (288°C).

7 When the cook time for the crisp is complete, open the lid and grasp the steam rack handles to carefully lift the rack and dish out of the pot.

8 Remove the foil cover and place the dish under the broiler for 1–2 minutes or until the topping turns golden brown. Remove the crisp from the oven and set aside to cool for at least 30 minutes.

9 While the crisp is cooling, make the whipped topping by adding the heavy cream and stevia extract to a medium bowl. Using an immersion blender, whip until stiff peaks are formed.

10 Using a slotted spoon, transfer the crisp to serving bowls. Top each serving with ½ tablespoon of the whipped cream. Serve warm.

SERVES: 6
SERVING SIZE: ⅔ CUP BERRY CRISP WITH ½ TBSP WHIPPED CREAM

PREP: 4 MINUTES
PRESSURE: 15 MINUTES
TOTAL: 55 MINUTES

SETTING: PRESSURE COOK
RELEASE: QUICK

4 cups frozen, unsweetened mixed berries (blueberries, blackberries, or raspberries)

⅔ cup erythritol and oligosaccharide blend granular sweetener, divided

1 tsp xanthan gum

⅔ cup almond flour

¼ cup unsweetened finely shredded coconut

½ tsp ground cinnamon

4 tbsp butter, melted

FOR THE TOPPING

⅓ cup heavy cream

¼ tsp stevia extract

tip *To make this recipe dairy-free, substitute 4 tbsp coconut oil for the butter and ⅓ cup coconut cream for the heavy cream.*

Nutrition per serving
CALORIES: 227 **FAT:** 18g **NET CARBS:** 7g **PROTEIN:** 2g

SERVES: 5
SERVING SIZE: 1 CAKE WITH 2 TBSP TOPPING

PREP: 6 MINUTES
PRESSURE: 9 MINUTES
TOTAL: 23 MINUTES

SETTING: PRESSURE COOK
RELEASE: QUICK

⅔ cup sugar-free, stevia-sweetened chocolate chips

½ cup butter

3 eggs

⅔ cup erythritol and oligosaccharide blend granular sweetener

¼ cup almond flour

1 tsp vanilla extract

FOR THE TOPPING

⅓ cup heavy cream

⅛ tsp stevia extract

tip *To make this recipe dairy-free, substitute ½ cup coconut oil for the butter and ⅓ cup full-fat coconut cream for the heavy cream.*

CHOCOLATE LAVA CAKES

The Instant Pot does an excellent job of creating dense and creamy cakes! These fudgy cakes are rich and decadent with a warm, creamy center. They're simply divine, but low in carbs and easy to prepare.

1 Spray five 6-ounce (170g) ramekins with nonstick coconut oil spray. Set aside.

2 Add the chocolate chips and butter to a medium saucepan and place over medium-low heat. Stirring continuously, heat until the ingredients are melted and combined and then remove the saucepan from heat. Set aside.

3 In a large bowl, combine the eggs, sweetener, almond flour, and vanilla extract. Whisk to combine.

4 Pour the melted chocolate mixture into the egg and flour mixture and mix thoroughly. Fill each ramekin half full with the cake batter.

5 Place the steam rack in the pot and add 1¾ cup water to the bottom of the pot.

6 Place three of the ramekins on top of the rack and then center the remaining two ramekins on top of the bottom ramekins.

7 Cover, lock the lid, and flip the steam release handle to the sealing position. Select **Pressure Cook (High)** and set the cook time for **9 minutes.**

8 While the cakes are cooking, make the whipped topping by combining the heavy cream and stevia extract in a medium bowl. Using an immersion blender or hand mixer, whip until stiff peaks are formed. Tightly cover with plastic wrap and transfer to the refrigerator to chill.

9 Once the cook time for cakes is complete, quick release the pressure, open the lid, and carefully transfer the ramekins to a cooling rack to set and cool for 7 minutes.

10 Once cooled, top each cake with 2 tbsp of the whipped topping. Serve warm.

Nutrition per serving
CALORIES: 420 **FAT:** 37g **NET CARBS:** 8g **PROTEIN:** 7g

VANILLA CHEESECAKE
with Fresh Strawberries

Luscious, sweet, and incredibly creamy, this sensational crust-free cheesecake features hints of vanilla and citrus. You'll quickly find that the Instant Pot makes a cheesecake with a fantastic creamy texture.

SERVES: 8
SERVING SIZE: 1 SLICE

PREP: 8 MINUTES
PRESSURE: 40 MINUTES
TOTAL: 10 HOURS 9 MINUTES

SETTING: PRESSURE COOK
RELEASE: NATURAL/QUICK

1 Place the steam rack in the inner pot and add 1½ cups water to the bottom of the pot. Cut out a round piece of parchment paper slightly larger than the bottom of a 7 x 3-inch (15.25 x 7.5cm) springform pan. Place the parchment paper in the bottom of the pan and fold the edges of the paper up onto the sides of the pan. Cut a round piece of aluminum foil slightly larger than the bottom of the pan and wrap the foil around the outside bottom of the pan.

2 Combine the cream cheese, heavy cream, sweetener, lemon juice, vanilla extract, and lemon zest in a large bowl. Using a hand mixer or stand mixer, blend the ingredients on medium until the mixture is creamy but still thick. Reduce the mixer speed to low and add the eggs one at a time. Mix until the ingredients are just combined.

3 Pour the cheesecake batter into the prepared pan. Place a paper towel over the top of the pan and then tightly wrap a sheet of aluminum foil over the paper towel. Fold a 20-inch (50cm) long piece of aluminum foil lengthwise and then into thirds to create a sling for easier removal of the pan. Place the pan in the center of the sling, grasp the ends and carefully lift and lower the pan into the pot.

4 Cover, lock the lid, and flip the steam release handle to the sealing position. Select **Pressure Cook (High)** and set the cook time for **40 minutes.**

5 While the cheesecake is cooking, make the sour cream topping by combining the sour cream and sweetener in a medium bowl. Whisk until blended. Set aside.

6 When the cook time for cheesecake is complete, allow the pressure to release naturally for 20 minutes and then quick release the remaining pressure. Open the lid and lift the cheesecake out of the pot. While the cheesecake is still warm, evenly spread the sour cream topping over top. Tightly cover and refrigerate for a minimum of 9 hours.

7 After the chilling time is complete, carefully release the outer spring ring of the springform pan to release the cheesecake from the pan. Cut into 8 equal-sized wedges. Garnish with the strawberries. Serve chilled.

16oz (450g) full-fat cream cheese, at room temperature

2 tbsp heavy cream

⅔ cup erythritol and oligosaccharide blend granular sweetener

1 tsp fresh lemon juice

1 tsp vanilla extract

1½ tsp freshly grated lemon zest

3 large eggs, at room temperature

⅓ cup sliced fresh strawberries

FOR THE TOPPING

½ cup full-fat sour cream

1 tbsp erythritol and oligosaccharide blend granular sweetener

tip *Only use block-style cream cheese for this recipe and not the whipped variety.*

Nutrition per serving
CALORIES: 275 **FAT:** 26g **NET CARBS:** 4g **PROTEIN:** 6g

SERVES: 6
SERVING SIZE: 1 PIECE

PREP: 6 MINUTES
PRESSURE: 44 MINUTES
TOTAL: 1 HOUR 30 MINUTES

SETTING: PRESSURE COOK
RELEASE: NATURAL/QUICK

⅓ cup grated carrots

⅓ cup grated zucchini

1 cup almond flour

⅔ cup erythritol and oligosaccharide blend granular sweetener

1 tsp baking powder

⅛ tsp baking soda

1 tsp ground cinnamon

½ tsp ground cardamom

¼ tsp grated nutmeg

2 large eggs

3 tbsp heavy cream

2 tbsp unsalted butter, melted

1 tsp vanilla extract

⅓ cup chopped walnuts

FOR THE FROSTING

4oz (110g) block-style cream cheese, softened and cubed

3 tbsp erythritol and oligosaccharide blend granular sweetener

2 tsp lemon juice

½ tsp vanilla extract

1 tbsp heavy cream

tip *This cake is preservative-free and perishable, so any leftovers must be refrigerated.*

CARROT CAKE
with Cream Cheese Frosting

Rich and moist, this keto-friendly spiced carrot cake features a decadent cream cheese frosting. Replacing half the grated carrot with grated zucchini helps lower the carbs without compromising the taste.

1 Spray a 6-inch (15.25cm) round cake pan with nonstick coconut oil spray. Set aside.

2 Line a large colander with paper towels and place the carrots and zucchini in the colander. Press down on the vegetables to force as much liquid from the vegetables as possible. Set aside.

3 Combine the almond flour, sweetener, baking powder, baking soda, cinnamon, cardamom, nutmeg, eggs, heavy cream, butter, and vanilla extract in a large bowl. Using a stand mixer or hand mixer, beat the ingredients on medium until thoroughly combined.

4 Pour the batter into the prepared pan and tightly cover the top of the pan with a sheet of aluminum foil.

5 Place the steam rack in the inner pot and add 1⅔ cups water to the bottom of the pot. Place the covered cake pan on the steam rack.

6 Cover, lock the lid, and flip the steam release handle to the sealing position. Select **Pressure Cook (High)** and set the cook time for **44 minutes.** When the cook time is complete, allow the pressure to release naturally for 10 minutes and then quick release the remaining pressure.

7 Open the lid and carefully grasp the steam rack handles to lift the rack and cake pan out of the pot. Remove and discard the aluminum foil and let the cake cool for 25–30 minutes.

8 While the cake is cooling, make the frosting by combining the cream cheese, sweetener, lemon juice, vanilla extract, and heavy cream in a large bowl. Using a hand mixer, beat the ingredients on high until well combined and a smooth, creamy consistency is achieved.

9 Once the cake is cool, spread the frosting over the top of the cake. Sprinkle the walnuts evenly over top.

10 Cut the cake into 8 equal-sized wedges. Serve promptly or transfer to a resealable container and refrigerate for up to 6 days.

Nutrition per serving
CALORIES: 248   **FAT:** 23g   **NET CARBS:** 4g   **PROTEIN:** 6g

SERVES: 8
SERVING SIZE: 1 SLICE

PREP: 10 MINUTES
PRESSURE: 55 MINUTES
TOTAL: 9 HOURS 15 MINUTES

SETTING: PRESSURE COOK
RELEASE: NATURAL/QUICK

16oz (450g) block-style,
full-fat cream cheese,
at room temperature

¾ cup erythritol and
oligosaccharide blend
granular sweetener

½ cup no-sugar-added
creamy peanut butter

2 tbsp full-fat sour cream

1 tsp vanilla extract

2 large eggs, at room temperature

1 egg yolk, at room temperature

FOR THE CHOCOLATE GANACHE

3oz (85g) unsweetened
baking chocolate

⅓ cup erythritol and
oligosaccharide blend
confectioner's powdered
sweetener

⅓ cup heavy cream

½ tsp vanilla extract

tip *Use only block-style
cream cheese for this recipe
and not the whipped variety.*

CHOCOLATE PEANUT BUTTER CHEESECAKE

Creamy, fluffy and utterly decadent, this crustless peanut butter cheesecake is drenched in a rich chocolate ganache to create a divine flavor combination. It tastes sinful, but it's low carb and keto!

1 Place a sheet of aluminum foil on a flat surface. Place a 7-inch (17.5cm) springform pan on the foil and tightly wrap the foil up and around the sides of the pan. Spray the inside of the pan with nonstick coconut oil spray and then line the inside bottom and sides with parchment paper.

2 Add the cream cheese and sweetener to a medium bowl. Using a stand mixer or hand mixer, beat on low until smooth and well combined. Scrape the sides with a rubber spatula. Add the peanut butter and continue mixing on low until a smooth consistency is achieved. Add the sour cream and vanilla and beat until smooth. Scrape the sides with a rubber spatula. Add the eggs and egg yolk and continue mixing on low until the ingredients are just blended.

3 Pour the batter into the prepared pan and tightly cover with aluminum foil. Add 1½ cups water to the inner pot. Place the pan on the steam rack and lower the rack and pan into the pot. Cover, lock the lid, and flip the steam release handle to the sealing position. Select **Pressure Cook (High)** and set the cook time for **55 minutes**. When the cook time is complete, allow the pressure to release naturally for 18 minutes and then quick release the remaining pressure.

4 Open the lid and carefully lift the rack and pan out of the pot. Remove the foil and gently blot the top of the cheesecake with a paper towel. Allow to cool for 20 minutes and then tightly cover and place in the refrigerator for a minimum of 8 hours. When the chilling time is complete, remove from the refrigerator and carefully remove the outer ring of the pan. Transfer the cheesecake to a serving platter.

5 Bring 1 inch (2.5cm) water to a simmer in a small saucepan. Place a tempered glass bowl over the mouth of the pan (the bottom of the bowl should not touch the water). Add the chocolate and heavy cream and heat until the chocolate is melted, stirring continuously. Remove the pan from the heat and stir in the vanilla. Carefully remove the bowl from the pan.

6 Starting at the outer edges of the cheesecake, pour the chocolate sauce over the cheesecake and continue toward the center. Cut into 8 equal-sized wedges. Serve promptly.

Nutrition per serving
CALORIES: 419   **FAT:** 36g   **NET CARBS:** 6g   **PROTEIN:** 10g

VANILLA BEAN CRÈME BRULEE

Creamy and velvety smooth, this keto-friendly crème brulee has accents of vanilla and a caramelized crust. It's a low-carb treat that is so simple to make in the Instant Pot!

SERVES: 4
SERVING SIZE: ⅓ CUP

PREP: 4 MINUTES
PRESSURE: 10 MINUTES
TOTAL: 4 HOURS 54 MINUTES

SETTING: PRESSURE COOK
RELEASE: NATURAL

1 Place the steam rack in the inner pot and add 2 cups cold water to the bottom of the pot.

2 In a large bowl, combine the egg yolks and sweetener. Whisk until the sweetener dissolves completely and then add the heavy cream, vanilla extract, and ground vanilla bean. Stir until combined.

3 Evenly divide the mixture between four 3-ounce (85g) ramekins and tightly cover each with a small piece of aluminum foil.

4 Arrange the ramekins on the steam rack in the pot. (One ramekin can be stacked on top of the others if all four will not fit on the rack.)

5 Cover, lock the lid, and flip the steam release handle to the sealing position. Select **Pressure Cook (High)** and set the cook time for **10 minutes.** When the cook time is complete, allow the pressure to release naturally (about 20 minutes).

6 Open the lid and carefully transfer the ramekins to a cooling rack. Discard the foil and let the ramekins cool to room temperature (about 30 minutes).

7 Tightly cover the cooled ramekins with plastic wrap and transfer to the refrigerator to chill for a minimum of 4 hours.

8 When the chilling time is complete, remove the ramekins from the refrigerator, uncover, and sprinkle 1 teaspoon of the sweetener over top of each ramekin.

9 Using a culinary torch, carefully melt the sweetener to form a caramelized crust. Alternatively, place the ramekins under an oven broiler at 550°F (288°C) for 4 minutes or until the sweetener begins to caramelize. (Watch carefully since the sweetener can burn very quickly.) Serve promptly.

3 egg yolks

3 tbsp erythritol granular sweetener

1 cup heavy cream

½ tbsp vanilla extract

⅛ tsp ground dried vanilla bean

4 tsp erythritol granular sweetener (for the caramelized crust)

tip *To make this recipe dairy-free, substitute 1 cup full-fat coconut milk for the heavy cream.*

A coffee grinder can be used to grind dried vanilla bean into a powder. (If you don't have dried vanilla bean, it can be omitted from the recipe.)

Nutrition per serving
CALORIES: 252 **FAT:** 25g **NET CARBS:** 2g **PROTEIN:** 3g

GIANT CHOCOLATE CHIP COOKIE

This giant cookie tastes just like a regular chocolate chip cookie, but it's sugar-free and low carb! Warm and gooey and filled with crunchy walnuts, this is the perfect keto-friendly sweet treat.

 SERVES: 8
SERVING SIZE: 1 SLICE

 PREP: 8 MINUTES
COOK: 4 HOURS
TOTAL: 4 HOURS 18 MINUTES

 SETTING: SLOW COOK
RELEASE: NONE

1. Line the inner pot with parchment paper and spray the paper with nonstick coconut oil spray. Set aside.

2. Add the sweetener and butter to a large bowl. Using a stand mixer or hand mixer, cream the butter and sweetener until thoroughly combined.

3. Add the egg, molasses, and vanilla extract. Continue to mix until thoroughly combined. Set aside.

4. In a separate large bowl combine the almond flour, coconut flour, baking powder, sea salt, and xanthan gum. Stir until blended.

5. Add the dry ingredients to the wet ingredients and mix until well combined. Fold in the chocolate chips and walnuts.

6. Add the cookie dough to the prepared inner pot. Using a rubber spatula, spread and press the dough into the bottom of the pot, making sure to cover the bottom completely and fill in any gaps.

7. Cover and lock the lid but leave the steam release handle in the venting position. Select **Slow Cook (High)** and set the cook time for 4 hours. When the cook time is complete, press **Cancel** to turn off the pot.

8. Open the lid and carefully transfer the inner pot with the cookie to a cooling rack. Allow the cookie to cool in the pot for a minimum of 30 minutes or until it reaches room temperature. (The cookie will look soft and doughy but will become firm as it cools.)

9. Transfer the cooled cookie to a serving plate and slice into 8 equal-sized wedges, or transfer to a resealable container and refrigerate for up to 6 days. Serve warm.

⅔ cup erythritol and oligosaccharide blend granular sweetener

5½ tbsp butter

1 large egg

1 tsp blackstrap molasses

½ tsp vanilla extract

1¼ cup almond flour

1 tbsp coconut flour

1½ tsp baking powder

⅛ tsp fine grind sea salt

½ tsp xanthan gum

½ cup sugar-free, stevia-sweetened chocolate chips

¼ cup chopped walnuts

tip *This cookie is preservative-free and perishable, so any leftovers must be refrigerated.*

Nutrition per serving
CALORIES: 210 **FAT:** 20g **NET CARBS:** 5g **PROTEIN:** 5g

SERVES: 6
SERVING SIZE: 1 CUPCAKE

PREP: 5 MINUTES
PRESSURE: 23 MINUTES
TOTAL: 40 MINUTES

SETTING: PRESSURE COOK
RELEASE: NATURAL/QUICK

¼ cup coconut flour

⅓ cup erythritol and oligosaccharide blend granular sweetener

1½ tsp pumpkin pie spice

1 tsp baking powder

½ tsp ground cinnamon

⅛ tsp fine grind sea salt

2 large eggs

¼ cup canned no-sugar-added pumpkin purée

2½ tbsp unsweetened almond milk

1 tsp vanilla extract

FOR THE FROSTING

4oz (110g) block-style cream cheese, softened and cubed

3 tbsp erythritol and oligosaccharide blend granular sweetener

1 tbsp heavy cream

1 tsp lemon juice

½ tsp vanilla extract

tip *To make this recipe dairy-free, substitute 4 oz (110g) vegetable shortening for the cream cheese and 1 tbsp coconut milk for the heavy cream.*

FROSTED PUMPKIN PIE CUPCAKES

Creamy and sweet with a soft pumpkin pie texture, these spiced cupcakes feature a lovely vanilla cream cheese frosting. They're a perfect low-carb treat that the whole family will love.

1 In a large bowl, combine the coconut flour, sweetener, pumpkin pie spice, baking powder, cinnamon, and sea salt. Stir to combine. Set aside.

2 In a medium bowl, combine the eggs, pumpkin purée, almond milk, and vanilla extract. Whisk until blended.

3 Make the batter by adding the wet ingredients to the dry ingredients and mixing until well combined. Set aside.

4 Add 1½ cups water to the bottom of the inner pot. Place a 10 x 10-inch (25cm x 25cm) sheet of aluminum foil over the steam rack.

5 Spoon the batter in equal amounts into 6 silicone muffin cups. Place the cups on the steam rack and fold the excess foil up and around the outside of the cupcakes. Grasp the rack handles and carefully lower the rack and cupcakes into the pot.

6 Place a second 10 x 10-inch (25cm x 25cm) sheet of aluminum foil loosely over the top of the cupcakes.

7 Cover, lock the lid, and flip the steam release handle to the sealing position. Select **Pressure Cook (High)** and set the cook time for **23 minutes.** When the cook time is complete, allow the pressure to release naturally for 10 minutes and then quick release the remaining pressure.

8 Open the lid and remove the aluminum foil cover. Grasp the rack handles to carefully lift the wrap and cupcakes out of the pot. Set the cupcakes aside to cool for 20 minutes.

9 While the cupcakes are cooling, make the frosting by combining the cream cheese, sweetener, heavy cream, lemon juice, and vanilla extract in a large bowl. Using a stand mixer or hand mixer, beat on medium speed until the frosting is smooth and creamy.

10 Once the cupcakes are cooled, spread equal amounts of the frosting over each cupcake. Serve promptly, or refrigerate in a resealable container for up to 6 days.

Nutrition per serving
CALORIES: 150   **FAT:** 11g   **NET CARBS:** 5g   **PROTEIN:** 5g

CHOCOLATE FUDGE BROWNIES

Dense, rich, and fudgy, these chocolatey brownies are low in carbs and oh-so-simple to make in the Instant Pot. This keto treat is perfect for those chocolate lovers who need their fix!

SERVES: 8
SERVING SIZE: 1 BROWNIE

PREP: 5 MINUTES
PRESSURE: 30 MINUTES
TOTAL: 55 MINUTES

SETTING: PRESSURE COOK
RELEASE: QUICK

1 In a medium bowl, combine the coconut flour, cocoa powder, sweetener, and sea salt. Mix well to combine.

2 In a separate medium bowl, combine the eggs, peanut butter, butter, vanilla extract, and melted baking chocolate. Stir to combine.

3 Add the wet ingredients to the dry ingredients and mix until combined. Add the chocolate chips and fold into the batter.

4 Generously coat the inside of a 6-inch (15.25cm) or 7-inch (17.5cm) cake pan with the olive oil. Line the bottom of the pan with a sheet of parchment paper cut into the shape of the bottom of the pan.

5 Pour the batter into the pan. Using a knife, spread the mixture into an even layer and then tightly cover the pan with a sheet of aluminum foil.

6 Add 1 cup water to the inner pot. Place the cake pan on the steam rack, grasp the steam rack handles, and carefully lower the rack and pan into the pot.

7 Cover, lock the lid, and flip the steam release handle to the sealing position. Select **Pressure Cook (High)** and set the cook time for **30 minutes.** When the cook time is complete, quick release the pressure.

8 Open the lid and grasp the steam rack handles to carefully lift the rack and pan out of the pot.

9 Tightly cover the pan with aluminum foil and place the brownies in the refrigerator to cool and set for a minimum of 20 minutes.

10 Once the brownies are set, remove from the pan and cut into 8 equal-sized pieces. Serve promptly.

2 tbsp coconut flour

3 tbsp unsweetened cocoa powder

1 cup erythritol and oligosaccharide blend granular sweetener

¼ tsp fine grind sea salt

2 large eggs

⅓ cup no-sugar-added creamy peanut butter

5 tbsp butter, melted

1 tsp vanilla extract

2oz (55g) unsweetened baking chocolate, melted

¼ cup sugar-free, stevia-sweetened chocolate chips

1 tbsp olive oil

tip *If desired, you can substitute ⅓ cup almond butter or ⅓ cup sunflower seed butter for the peanut butter.*

Nutrition per serving
CALORIES: 300 **FAT:** 20g **NET CARBS:** 3g **PROTEIN:** 25g

INDEX

Publisher Mike Sanders
Senior Editor Brook Farling
Book Designer Rebecca Batchelor
Art Director William Thomas
Photographer Daniel Showalter
Food Stylist Savannah Norris
Proofreader Monica Stone
Indexer Celia McCoy

First American Edition, 2019
Published in the United States by DK Publishing
6081 E. 82nd Street, Indianapolis, Indiana 46250

Copyright © 2019 Dorling Kindersley Limited
DK, a Division of Penguin Random House LLC
19 20 21 22 23   10 9 8 7 6 5 4 3 2 1
001–312952–January/2019

Published in the United States by Dorling Kindersley Limited

Note: This publication contains the opinions and ideas of its author(s).
It is intended to provide helpful and informative material on the subject
matter covered. It is sold with the understanding that the author(s) and
publisher are not engaged in rendering professional services in the
book. If the reader requires personal assistance or advice, a competent
professional should be consulted. The author(s) and publisher
specifically disclaim any responsibility for any liability, loss, or risk,
personal or otherwise, which is incurred as a consequence, directly or
indirectly, of the use and application of any of the contents of this book.

Trademarks: All terms mentioned in this book that are known to be
or are suspected of being trademarks or service marks have been
appropriately capitalized. Alpha Books, DK, and Penguin Random
House LLC cannot attest to the accuracy of this information. Use of
a term in this book should not be regarded as affecting the validity
of any trademark or service mark.

INSTANT POT® and associated logos are owned by Instant Brands Inc.
and used under license.

A catalog record for this book
is available from the Library of Congress.
ISBN 978-1-4654-8073-6
Library of Congress Catalog Number: 2018952586

DK books are available at special discounts when purchased
in bulk for sales promotions, premiums, fund-raising, or educational
use. For details, contact: DK Publishing Special Markets, 345 Hudson
Street, New York, New York 10014
SpecialSales@dk.com

Printed and bound in China

All images © Dorling Kindersley Limited
For further information see: www.dkimages.com

A WORLD OF IDEAS:
SEE ALL THERE IS TO KNOW

www.dk.com